John Allyn

A Sketch of Matthew Allyn and his Descendants to 1884

Also, Selections of the prose Publications of John Allyn and his poetic writings

John Allyn

A Sketch of Matthew Allyn and his Descendants to 1884

Also, Selections of the prose Publications of John Allyn and his poetic writings

ISBN/EAN: 9783337078348

Printed in Europe, USA, Canada, Australia, Japan

Cover: Foto ©ninafisch / pixelio.de

More available books at **www.hansebooks.com**

OF

MATTHEW ALLYN

AND

HIS DESCENDANTS TO 1884.

ALSO, SELECTIONS OF THE PROSE PUBLICATIONS OF

JOHN ALLYN,

AND HIS POETIC WRITINGS.

SAN FRANCISCO:
A. L. BANCROFT & CO., PRINTERS.

1884.

PREFACE.

This work is not intended to interest the general public or to be put on sale. Its object is to rescue from oblivion and hand down to posterity such fragments as may be had of the lives of Matthew Allyn. the first settler known in America, and his descendants.

I am indebted for a great portion of the information embodied in this work to sketches by Mary L. Hart, published in the Winsted *Herald*. Besides putting these fragments in convenient form, I wish to perpetuate such selections of my published prose writings as may be thought worth preservation, and also my poetic writings entire— good, bad, and indifferent—with a few favorite selections. Without apologizing, I will state that, after a busy life, I commenced writing this poetry at the age of fifty-seven, leaving the reader to estimate their quality. It has all been published in local periodicals, and some quoted, from one side of the continent to the other.

INDEX.

	PAGE.
Matthew Allyn and his Descendants, - -	9
Will and Morals, - - - - - - -	38
Scientific Indications of Progression, - - - -	94
The Coming Religion, - - - - - -	113
Experience with Spirits, - - - - - -	137
Poems, - - - - - - - -	142
Essay on Woman Suffrage, - - - - -	169
Miscellaneous, - - - - - - -	176

A SKETCH
—OF—
MATTHEW ALLYN
—AND—
HIS DESCENDANTS TO 1884.

MATTHEW ALLYN. *see front of*

Of Matthew Allyn, the first settler of the name in America, little is known but that he settled in Windsor, in Connecticut. Nothing whatever is known of the family previous to emigration from England. The name seems to indicate Welsh origin. I have nothing to relate until we come to Pelatiah Allyn, Jr., the first settler of Barkhamsted, Litchfield Co., Conn. His story I give as told by Mary L. Hart, of Barkhamsted.

PELATIAH ALLYN, Jr.

Time ever speeds onward, and in its ceaseless course the march of civilization presses forward to uncultivated regions, where the red man and the wild beast have long held undisputed sway. And thus it was when Barkhamsted was an unbroken wilderness, when the mountain-tops and the valleys were alike a dense and unsubdued forest; when the deer roamed at will; when the panther, the bear and the wolf made the night hideous with their wild and savage outcries.

Such a region would seem to hold little in its embrace to allure or invite settlers to make a home, for well must they be aware of the hardships and privations to which they must be subjected.

At the first settlement of Connecticut it was natural that the most accessible portions should have been chosen, and that the lovely and fertile Connecticut Valley should first be selected and cultivated. As the incoming tides brought an increase of population the domains expanded, and emigration pushed westward, until the rocky and mountainous regions of Barkhamsted were reached, and though it was less inviting than many other localities, yet one man had the energy, the perseverance and stamina requisite to fell the lofty trees and commence a settlement within the wilderness, and lay the corner-stone for the future growth and prosperity of the town, which has for more than a century been famous upon the pages of history. To this man, and the work of his hands, and the record which he has left behind after the coming and going of these many years, would I invite the attention of my readers, with regret and sorrow that I cannot lift the veil which shadows his life and give an accurate and full description of the pioneer settler of our town. The grave has long held his sacred ashes, and his memory lives in the hearts of his great-grandchildren, and like that grave in the land of Moab, on Nebo's lonely mountain, "no man knoweth of his sepulchre unto this day."

The first white settler in the town of Barkhamsted was Pelatiah Allyn, Jr., who came from Windsor, Conn., and was the son of Pelatiah Allyn, who was descended from Matthew Allyn, the first of the family that came from England to this country.

Pelatiah Allyn of Windsor, deeded land lying in the town of Barkhamsted "in an unbroken state" to his son Pelatiah, Jr., who came to this town in 1746, and built a log house about one mile north of New Hartford, on the ridge which divides the east branch of the Farmington river from the west branch.

He was at this time unmarried, and many vague stories have been handed down of hardships and discouragements, of encounters with the wild beasts of the forest, as well as with the red man. Tradition has it that before he built his log-house he had a large box secured with iron bands in which he used to sleep nights, and one day after becoming much fatigued, he lay down in his box to rest, and in some unaccountable manner the lid of the box fell down, which fastened with a spring, and for the same length of time that Jonah was confined in his close quarters did Mr. Allyn remain a prisoner, and when nearly dead was released by a party of hunters, who in their meanderings in quest of game discovered a coat hanging on a tree close by, and were led to gratify their curiosity regarding the box and its contents by an investigation, which resulted most happily for Mr. Allyn, and for the future good and prosperity of this town.

From a letter written by Rev. Ozias Eells, the first settled minister of this town, to Dr. Trumbull, the historian, we find that at the time of his coming there was considerable disturbance from the Indians in New Hartford and the region round about, and the alarm became so great that at the north end of New Hartford they had a house "forted in," to which all the families went to lodge, and were obliged to work their fields in companies, with their fire-arms. Mr. Allyn became alarmed, and felt so insecure that he went and lodged with them—and that my readers may understand his situation I will copy a small portion of Parson Eells' letter, which is published in full in the Barkhamsted Centennial Book, compiled by William Wallace Lee, of Meriden:

"Mr. Allyn, finding he must be alone in the day-time or leave his place, concluded to secure himself as well as he could. He had built him a house with one large room and a small room for his bed. Just before the door that led into his bedroom, about one small step, he had a trap-door which led into his cellar. At night he used to lay things around his outside door that a noise might be made if any one came to get into the house, and then shut his bedroom door and raised his trap-door, which opened from the bedroom door, that if they entered there they must fall into the cellar, and in this way he lived for some years unmarried, and never met with any disturbance from the Indians."

His wife's name was Sarah Moody, she being a resident of New Hartford, and daughter of Adonijah Moody. They were married about 1751 or '52. Pelatiah Allyn, Jr., was born in Windsor in 1713. *Oct 4, 1714*

Pelatiah Jr. and Sarah his wife had but one son, who was born in 1755, and to whom they gave the family name of Pelatiah, which is a Bible name found in Ezekiel xi. 1, 13. A daughter was born to them, but I do not find the date of her birth, although she lived to marry, of which we will speak hereafter.

Pelatiah 2d owned a large tract of land in this town, including several hundred acres. After he was on the downhill of life he became embarrassed in debt and shut himself in his house. One morning he found a pane of glass removed and a gun lay under the window, which he inferred was placed by some friend to let him know his danger. He owned a slave, a black woman by the name of Lily, and as she was property and could be taken for debt they hid her up stairs in a deep hole down by the chimney. She fell to Pelatiah 3d, and afterwards married and had one or two children.

A fine buff vest, sent with other goods from England in payment of Pelatiah 2d's share of a fortune in Indian bonds, is in the possession of one of his great-grandsons. Some historians claim that Pelatiah Allyn 2d settled first in New Hartford, and that the records of that town show when land was deeded by himself and Sarah Moody, his wife, to the town, but this was doubtless land first owned by the father of Sarah Moody, but the land of Pelatiah 2d is said to have lain partly in New Hartford.

My information of the first settler is derived chiefly from family tradition, and may be in many respects incorrect. He died at the age of 70 in the year 1783. In our next chapter we will take the life of Pelatiah 3d, who was the only son of the pioneer settler of Barkhamsted.

The writer of this paragraph, J. Allyn, was born on said farm, a small part of which is over the line in New Hartford. In his youth he made hay many a day in a field which was part in New Hartford and part in Barkhamsted.

PELATIAH ALLYN, 3d.

Pelatiah, son of Pelatiah 2d and Sarah Moody, his wife, was born in 1755, and married Mary Ann Gillett, an aunt of Matthew Gillett and also of Ann Gillett, who became the wife of Joseph Wilder. Mary Ann Gillett was born in 1758. They had three sons, Pelatiah, Henry, and Matthew.

When Pelatiah 3d was a young man he was consumptive and afflicted for years with a bronchial cough. He had in later years fever sores on both of his limbs, and there is living at present an aged lady who, when a child, lived in his family and can remember, as though it were but yesterday, seeing him dress his limbs, daily bathing them in mineral water, rolling and unrolling the bandages.

He is described as a kind and most agreeable man, enjoying hugely a joke or laughable incident. He was of spare habits, of few words, and quite a mathematician. His ambition often went far beyond his strength. His death was occasioned by persisting in plowing his cornfield during a very warm day of May, 1815, while his hired help were hoeing the same. A man by the name of Pike, thinking he overestimated his strength, urged him to let him take the plow, but he refused. His death occurred May 21, 1815, at 60 years of age.

A favorite maxim of his was, to "live as though we were to live forever, or die to-morrow." A slab in the old cemetery marks the last resting-place of Pelatiah 3d, and the visitors to that silent but sacred city "over the river and on the hill" will read from the moss-grown slab the words which have been carved for many a year, "Blessed are the dead who die in the Lord, for their works do follow them."

He represented the town in the State legislature twenty-two times, going the last time in 1814. One anecdote of his is given as authentic. The Indians as a class are fond of having a "paper," as they called it, which should serve to introduce them and gain favors and odd jobs of work from the people. At the most earnest solicitation of an Indian, Captain Allyn prepared a paper which read thus: "The bearer of this is a tolerable good Indian. He does his work well; but if you have any hatchets or tools of any kind lying around loose look out for him, as he will steal anything he can lay his hands on." This Indian could not read, and he took great pride in presenting the paper of recommendation to the white people and soliciting favors.

Before the incorporation of the town, which took place in October, 1779, a military company was organized here, in October, 1774. Pelatiah 3d was chosen captain. From traditional repute we learn that this company were inexperienced in military tactics, and they did not obey the captain's order to "Right about face!" in an approved manner, and with patience nearly exhausted he succeeded in getting them in line again, when, with a loud voice, he gave the command, "Wheel! Wheel to my son Pelatiah on the fence!" which command was quickly and most gracefully obeyed.

On one occasion a neighbor made some wooden combs which did not require any great amount of mechanical ingenuity, but which he displayed with a vast amount of pride to his neighbor, Captain Allyn. Taking the coarse, awkward, red-painted combs in his hand, the captain, after a careful inspection, told him "they would make quite respectable oven wood."

As the aged lady, with the weight of more than fourscore years resting upon her, with fingers tremulous with age unlocks the door of the hidden Past and lives in memory amid the scenes of childhood and all its tender and sacred associations; and when but a child of eight years she enters the dwelling of Pelatiah and Mary Allyn, and spreads before us a panorama of the familiar scenes, introduces us to those who were indeed her parents, tenderly caresses the faces which were so dear to her through years of her girlhood, we can but marvel that the mind should after the lapse of so many years recall so much of what has been, and with eyes dimmed by the coming and going of so many eventides see again the prancing iron-gray colt led to the horse-block, Captain Allyn mounted, guiding and controlling the fiery animal by the sound of his own voice, while the reins lie upon his neck. Again she sees the family at church, sitting in a square, high-backed pew in the old meeting-house, a part of the pew being occupied by Colonel Israel Jones and wife, who, as long as she can remember, sat with them until their number was lessened by the beckoning of the Death Angel.

From his elevated position in the great high pulpit she sees Parson Eells, from Sunday to Sunday, as a loved and reverend shepherd, feeding the lambs of his flock. Within the sacred precincts of home she sees Mrs. Allyn, attired in short gown and petticoat, industriously working at her loom carding and weaving, while she herself fills the quills.

About a mile from Mr. Allyn's lived a man by the name of Michael ———, who came from Scotland and was by trade a weaver and proficient in the art. He was fond of cider, and would often go to Mr. Allyn's and tell the little maid that if she would draw some cider he would fill the quills for her. The work of filling the quills was quite distasteful to the young girl and she would gladly make the exchange; and while he was engaged in performing his part of the stipulation he would sing some pleasing song, and often would beg for "a crust of bread for his stomach's sake." His wife was peculiar and strange in appearance, walking much like a person intoxicated, and associated but little with the people about them. She owned land, and one time a man cut some trees on her property and she went to Captain Allyn in her trouble.

Mrs. Rockwell, on Center Hill, used to comb wool to spin for worsted, which was made into cloth, stockings and gloves, and Mrs. Allyn used to send her wool to Mrs. Rockwell to have it combed. Rebecca Pike, a maiden lady, used to spin for Mrs. Allyn, and she would say she had rather be with her than anywhere else. She was about Mrs. Allyn's age, and was a very amiable and social person. She had the misfortune to fall into a kettle of boiling porridge when she was small and was fearfully burned, and although she lived she was never strong and healthy, and was diminutive in stature.

When Captain Allyn lived in the old house, in the dining-room there was a long bench on one side of the table for the men to sit upon, it being longer than the table. Captain Allyn sat at the end of the table and his dog Hunter would sit by his side on the end of the bench and the 'Squire would feed him; and when Hunter did not receive the attention to which he thought he was entitled he would place his paw on the 'Squire's arm, when his wants would be supplied.

In the latter part of Captain Allyn's life he became quite deaf, and Dr. Amos Beecher used to go often to see him. One day while there he extracted with his turnkeys the first tooth this little girl was called upon to part with; and now the remembrance of that incident is fresh in the evening of her life.

The daughter of the pioneer and Sarah Moody, his wife, married a man by the name of Shepard, and she died leaving a babe, which she gave to her brother, Captain Allyn. She left a will, though how much land she owned is not known. She left also a silk dress for her daughter Polly, which she did not wear until her marriage, in 1806, with Sylvester Jones, who had lived with 'Squire Allyn for some time previous.

PELATIAH ALLYN, 4th.

Pelatiah Allyn 4th, oldest son of Captain Pelatiah Allyn, was born December 4, 1785. He married Amelia Taylor, a daughter of Ozias Taylor, of Canton, January 14, 1808. Amelia Taylor was born April 19, 1785. They lived in Barkhamsted, on the west side of the Farmington river, below Cannon's Forge. Here they were richly blessed by the birth of seven children, four sons and three daughters, viz.: Mary Ann, Pelatiah, jr., Amelia, Ozias, William H. Walter and Chestina. Mary Ann was born May 10, 1809; Pelatiah, jr., September 8, 18.0; Amelia, July 14, 1812; Ozias, September 30, 1814; William H., April 4, 1817; Walter, February 23, 1819; Chestina, May 29, 1821.

Pelatiah 4th had long cherished a desire to see the "far west," as Ohio was then called, and he consulted with his father regarding the matter, who said to him, "No doubt Ohio has good land, but it has no market, and never can have, since it is an inland State." His anxiety to see the much heard of land of promise increased, however, and in 1819 he set out on horseback to see that remote country.

His father-in-law had settled in Ohio, at Worthington, near Columbus, and after a ride of sixteen or eighteen days he reached his home. He was much pleased with the country, but thought the climate must be bad, as the countenances of the family he noticed were a trifle sallow.

From there he set out for "New Connecticut," or what is now known as the "Western Reserve," which comprises some thirteen counties in the north-east part of the State. While on his journey, he came one evening, not far from the hour of sunset, to the dismal, solitary house of a settler, and from him gained the intelligence that the next house was twenty miles distant. Being rather anxious to reach his destination, he resolved to push on, but darkness settled upon the path before him; he was unable to keep the narrow track marked only by blazed trees, and he was reluctantly forced to halt until the rising of the moon should light him on his way with her friendly beams. In the distance he heard the dismal howl of a pack of wolves, and in a state of much disquiet became aware of their near approach. His thoughts worked with the speed of lightning, and the one in predominance was how he could save himself, and that was easily done by climbing a tree, but, alas! his poor horse would be killed and devoured by the eager, hungry pack, and he could not well afford to lose this faithful beast, and manfully resolved to fight them off. Accordingly he cut a large club and stood in defense ready to give them some sore heads ere they should secure their expected prey.

With gleaming eyes and hungry looks the wolves advanced nearer and nearer, and as the valiant little man fearlessly stood his ground they went around him howling dismally, not daring to attack him, and now, as the queen of night sails majestically up and lights the scene, they left him unmolested, and he was able to resume his journey, reaching the house he was in quest of before night folded her starry mantle.

After viewing the "New Connecticut" he started for home, where he arrived after a twelve days' journey. He was much pleased with the country, but not until the spring of 1822 could he get his wife to consent to "go west" to Ohio and leave their Barkhamsted home. In six weeks after gaining her consent they were on the road with two yoke of oxen, one large wagon, one one-horse wagon, one cow and one horse. Nelson Gilbert, son of Asa Gilbert, went with them and his expenses were borne for the assistance he was enabled to render.

They left Barkhamsted in the month of June, during the early part of the month, and were four weeks on the road. They did not make any permanent settlement until the following August. Three more children were added to the number in their new home—Watson, Orson, and Orville—and these were born in Hiram, Portage county. Watson was born June 4, 1824; Orson, July 25, 1826; and Orville, March 10, 1829.

Pelatiah was a successful and well-to-do farmer, and lived to see his promise verify itself, in giving to each of his children, ten in number, one hundred acres of land. As to his personal appearance, he was about five feet ten inches in height, with light hair, blue eyes, and a round red face. His figure was somewhat plump and round, and he was not an imposing-looking man. He was a wiry, sinewy man, whose muscles never tired, and whose endurance knew no limit.

He was ambitious and hopeful, ever eager for the unborn to-morrow, with new plans and new hopes.

With "never say die" for his motto, he knew no such word as fail.

Amelia Taylor, his wife, was a tall, bony woman, with great powers of endurance. She was six feet in height, and in her prime weighed two hundred pounds. She was a person who knew her own mind and could speak it plainly when occasion required. She was a most kind and indulgent mother, and as she grew feeble and aged, with one voice her children could "rise up and call her blessed."

She and her husband both lived to see the day when Ohio had a market and was fast assuming its place among the first States of the Union. They lived to enjoy its rapid growth and prosperity, and with pleasure and appreciation of Invention's mighty march journeyed over the iron roads of their adopted State, in strong contrast to the way in which they entered its limits, with their carts drawn by slow plodding oxen. Pelatiah Allyn 4th died December 18, 1856; Amelia Taylor, his wife, September 13, 1867. The former died from paralysis, to which the Allyn family have a tendency, the descendants fearing that disease more than any other.

Pelatiah and Amelia Allyn had ten children, four of whom are now living; grandchildren, 56, 34 of whom are living; great-grandchildren, 51, 38 of whom are living. Mary Ann, the oldest child, married, January, 1827, James I. Young, who was by occupation a farmer. She had ten children, four of whom are living; 13 grandchildren, ten of whom are living. She died February 27, 1852.

Pelatiah, the oldest son, was by trade a carpenter. March 12, 1835, he married Adeline Joslin, by whom he had eight children, four living at present. Of his eleven grandchildren, all are living. He died March 5, 1852.

Amelia Allyn married John Mason, July 14, 1812, he being by occupation a farmer. She had nine children and four grandchildren. Seven children are living and three grandchildren. She died September 9, 1882. Her husband lives at Trenton, Missouri.

Ozias Allyn married Caroline Norton, May, 1838, by whom he had two children, both now dead. September 30, 1844, he married Anna Norton, and four children blessed this union and are still living. Ozias was a farmer. He died May 18, 1883, from paralysis, he being a resident of Hiram, Ohio.

William H. Allyn married, October, 1837, Sarah Ann Slayton, and had nine children and three grandchildren. Five children are living and one grandchild. He is by trade a carpenter, and lives in Hardin county, Ohio.

Watson Allyn married, in 1837, Roxy M. Pinney, and had only one child, which is dead. He died in August, 1874. He was a merchant. His widow resides in Ridgeway, Hardin county, Ohio.

Chestina Allyn was married, June 2, 1842, to E. M. Young, and resides in Hiram, Ohio, and is the wife of a carpenter. They have three children and two grandchildren.

Watson Allyn married, November, 1849, Hattie Vaugh; October 24, 1857, Eunice Clark; and April 12, 1876, Rosella Udall. He had two children by his first wife, one by the second, which is dead, and two by the third wife, one of which is living. He has one grandchild. He has a wonderful mechanical genius and is "Jack at all trades." His home is in Portage county, Ohio.

Orson Allyn married Elvira King in 1856, and had two children and five grandchildren. He was a carpenter, and died in November, 1874.

Orville Allyn, in January, 1855, married Lorinda E. Young, and had three children, one of which died. He is a farmer, and lives in Lucas county, Ohio.

All of Pelatiah and Amelia Allyn's children were members of the same church of which President Garfield was a member when he died. They have been prominent men and women wherever they have settled, of strong and energetic character.

Three of Pelatiah and Amelia's grandchildren are college graduates, Sutton E. and Clark M. Young, children of Chestina Allyn Young, and Frank P., son of William H. Allyn. They are graduates of Hiram College, of which President Garfield was once both pupil and president.

Only one of Pelatiah and Amelia's children ever taught school, which is worthy of mention, that one being Watson, who taught for a considerable period in his younger days.

Four of the grandchildren of Pelatiah and Amelia came to violent deaths. Aaron, son of Ozias, was killed in the army; Kate, a daughter of Ozias, was thrown from a wagon and injured so that she lived only a few hours; Allen Young, son of Mary Ann Allen Young, and William Mason,

son of Amelia Allyn Mason, were both killed by an overdose of morphine.

In our late war this family furnished five brave soldiers, but only one came out alive. Edwin, son of Pelatiah 5th, died of disease in the army; Aaron, son of Ozias, was shot at Port Gibson; Elijah, son of Amelia Mason, died of wounds received in battle, as did also Homer, son of William H. Allyn. He also sent his son Alvin, who returned unharmed and is still living.

There seems to be an abundance of teachers in this branch of the family, as Pelatiah 5th has a son and daughter, Edward and Mary, who are teachers, as also were Fred, Sarah, Amelia, children of Amelia Allyn Mason; Kate, Aaron, Minnie, Emma, and Henry, children of Ozias; Mollie and Frank P., children of William Allyn; Rena A., Sutton E. and Clark M., children of Chestina Allyn Young. She also has a son, Sutton E., who is a lawyer. He was also elected to the State legislature, and was formerly of Kenton, Ohio.

Among all this long list of names of the grandchildren of Pelatiah and Amelia Allyn no disciple of Esculapius can be found, which seems somewhat singular.

Of family relics, Watson Allyn has a compass which was owned by his great-grandfather, Pelatiah 2d; a brass kettle bought during the war of 1812 by his father, and also a chain bought by him in 1820, and when he went to Ohio in 1822 he carried a broad-ax, on which is stamped plainly at the present day the name of Elijah Cannon.

Chestina Allyn Young has a bible that bears her mother's maiden name, Amelia Taylor, in it, and the date of her marriage.

Pelatiah Allyn 4th was the second person with a family that moved into Freedom Township, Ohio, at that time a wilderness. Captain Payne was the first settler. One day in the fall of 1832, Captain Payne and Pelatiah Allyn shouldered their muskets and started off hunting. Captain Payne being a great hunter. They soon ran a cub up a tree, and Captain Payne, bringing his gun to his shoulder, took deliberate aim and fired, and down came the cub, crying so loudly when attacked by the dogs that the mother bear appeared upon the scene quite unceremoniously and fought desperately for her babe—bear, cub, and dogs all in a pile. Mr. Allyn went up close to try to shoot the bear and save the dogs, when the bear came for him and when within six or eight feet of him he snapped his gun, which missed fire, and Captain Payne, in telling the story later, said "his hair at that stage of affairs stood straight up," as he expected he should be forced to use his rifle as a club, but Mr. Allyn did not move, but raised his gun and waited for the beast to attack him, but she ran the other way instead, and they were glad to dispense with her company.

HENRY ALLYN.

Henry Allyn, second son of Pelatiah 3d and Mary Ann Gillett, was born April 1, 1792. He married October 14, 1813, Sophia Taylor, daughter of Ozias Taylor of Canton, she being a sister of his brother Pelatiah's wife. He lived in the house on the road south of where 'Squire John Merrell lived, the house for the past few years being owned and occupied by the late George T. Carter.

They had nine children: Clarinda, Clarissa, Evaline, Henry, Hiram, Sophia, Homer, Caroline, and Helen. All his children were born in this town with the exception of the youngest daughter, Helen.

In June, 1835, Henry Allyn moved to Ohio with his entire family, with one exception. His oldest daughter remained in Barkhamsted. He was accompanied by his brother Matthew and his family, and also by his mother. Their first stopping place was with the brother who had preceded them in Hiram, Portage county, an account of whose journey west and life thereafter has been given above. Henry first took land and fitted a home in Freedom, Portage county; afterwards he removed to Wellington, where some of the family still live.

Clarinda, the oldest daughter, was born in 1814, and was married September 10, 1834, to Daniel J. Rexford, a son of John Rexford of Center Hill, and lived in Barkhamsted until a few years ago when they moved to Stamford, New York. They had seven children: Emily, Orlo, Henry, Eva, Ellen, Lizzie, and Mary.

Emily married Sheldon Johnson son of Ralph Johnson, of Center Hill. She died leaving one child, a son. His death was caused by sliding down hill lying face downwards upon his sled, which ran against a tree—his head striking the tree and he was instantly killed.

Orlo married Miss Susan Paddleford of Colebrook, and at present is a resident of Winsted and a man much respected. He has several children.

Henry married Miss Jennette Guernsey, daughter of Joseph B. Guernsey of Barkhamsted, and at once left his young and fair bride for the toils and hardships of a soldier's life. He enlisted August 21, 1862, in Company E, 2d Artillery, and was killed at Cold Harbor, June 1, 1864.

Eva is a noted school-teacher, teaching for a number of years in Barkhamsted and vicinity; later in Winsted, where she had a private school, and since their removal to New York State she has taught in several of the western States and meets with success.

Ellen married before they left Barkhamsted a Mr. Gibbs of New York State, and at present resides at Pittsburg, Penn., Mr. Gibbs forming one of the firm of T. H. Nevius & Co. of that place. They have several children.

Lizzie is a graduate of Vassar College and a teacher. She married a gentleman by the name of Graves, who also is a teacher.

Mary is a graduate of Mount Holyoke Seminary, South Hadley, and teaches in the same school with Mr. and Mrs. Graves. They are a superior family and have had fine educational advantages. Mrs. Rexford is a cultured and refined lady.

Clarissa Allyn was born in 1818, and married Cornelius Johnson, M. D. He died leaving two daughters. She married John Gill; he died and left two sons and two daughters. She died October 5, 1869, aged 51 years.

Evaline Allyn, born in 1820, married Miles Saxton, who died several years since, leaving her with three daughters and one son. They reside in Olivet, Michigan.

Henry Allyn, born in 1823, married Nancy Mason and died December, 1878, aged 55, leaving a widow and three daughters in Hiram, Ohio.

Hiram Allyn went to Ohio with his parents when but ten years of age. At twenty-five years of age he married Miss Elizabeth Merrell, a daughter of Samuel Merrell of Barkhamsted, who had previously moved west to Galena, Illinois, where his wife died, and on his return to Connecticut he stopped to visit his sister—the wife of Matthew Allyn. Hiram Allyn and Elizabeth Merrell had always attended school together in Barkhamsted until they were separated by the removal west. They were born the same year, the same month, but not quite the same day, and they were not slow in renewing the friendship of their childhood days. When Hiram saw the little girl of ten years had grown into a handsome and attractive young lady, all the love he had felt for the little school girl who had met him daily at the school-house, romped with him hand in hand on the green at recess, studied from the same book, recited in the same class, returned ten-fold, and he found occasion soon to tell to the sweet-faced Elizabeth the old, old story:

> "I am strong and you are weak,
> Life is but a slippery steep,
> Hung with shadows cold and deep.
> Will you trust me, Katie dear,
> Walk beside me without fear?
> May I carry, if I will,
> All your burdens up the hill?"

And like the Katie we read in the sweet old poem:

> " * * she answered with a laugh,
> No, but you may carry half."

So Hiram saved a long trip to Connecticut to woo the fair girl, and they were wed, and now after the sunlight and shades of many years, this same Hiram, far down life's walk, out of the fullness of his heart sends greetings to the author of Barkhamsted Reminiscences, and doubts if in the wide world so good wives and mothers can be found as have been reared among the hills and valleys of Barkhamsted, and enthusiastically calls God's blessing to rest upon his native town.

They have had eight children—five sons and three daughters. Emily, the eldest, is married and lives in Iowa. The next were twin boys, but only one is living, who is married, and whose present residence is in Portage county. Kittie, the second daughter, died at four years of age. Arthur, Fred, Jennie, and Walter all live at home.

Elizabeth Merrell Allyn came to Barkhamsted in 1880, during the month of September, accompanied by Mr. and Mrs. Saxton (née Mary Allyn, daughter of Matthew). She still retains the pleasant and pleasing expression which characterized her when a girl.

Hiram Allyn now lives at Wellington, Ohio, and his history seemed somewhat checkered, he being one of the restless, roving natures, who thinks " variety the spice of life " and must have change to break the monotony of every-day life. He retains pleasing recollections of his native town and has always been proud of it, doubtless because he left when he was a small lad. His memory is remarkably well preserved in many respects for a boy of ten years, as he in imagination sees the school-house at the Center; the teacher with uplifted hemlock whip descending upon his defenseless head and back—reminding him most vividly of his short-comings; the old meeting-house, " the most romantic of all," the lofty pulpit where the ministers gave to saint and sinner their portion in due season, even as the great Father-heart, out of its abundance, sends rain on the just and on the unjust; the little brook that summer and winter went dancing and chattering down its rocky channel, where in summer the boys made a dam and shut frogs and small fish in its keeping, and all the many events of his childhood's days are deeply impressed on the mind of the man of to-day in his Ohio home.

Sophia Allyn, born in 1828, lived in Wellington and married Frank Lewis. She died November 11, 1853, leaving two children, a son and daughter.

——— Allyn, born in 1834, married Joseph Snow, who died, leaving her with two children. She then married a Mr. Shumway and died in Michigan, leaving one child.

Helen Lucretia Allyn was born in Ohio in 1837, married William Saxton and has eight children, and now lives in Humboldt county, Iowa.

Sophia Taylor Allyn died August 4, 1852, aged 59.

In March, 1853, Henry Allyn married Mrs. Louisa Tiffany, widow of Timothy Tiffany, whose maiden name was Louisa Hart, she being second daughter of Josiah Hall Hart. Mr. Allyn lived with this second wife seven years and di d August 3, 1860, aged 68 years and 4 months. His widow then went to Detroit, Michigan, to live with a son.

There is a tradition in the families who spell their name Allyn that two brothers came from England and located in Windsor, and one of them wishing to distinguish his progeny spelled his name differently from the old familiar way, he spelling that of himself and family Allyn, while his brother still retained the old way of Allen, and in this way their descendants could be readily traced.

MATTHEW ALLYN.

Matthew Allyn, the third son of Pelatiah and Mary Ann Allyn, was born April 16, 1794. He married Clara Merrell, daughter of John Merrell, who was born October 12, 1794. They were married May 8, 1816. They lived at the old homestead, which was a large, old-fashioned house, and here nine children were born—Matthew Jr., Mark, John, James, Mary, Pelatiah, Phineas, George, and Ann. They commenced naming their children Bible names—Matthew, Mark (skipping Luke), John, etc. When they used to attend school on the green the boys would call, "Matthew, Mark, Luke, and John, take a stick and tuck it on."

In 1835 Mr. Allyn sold his farm in Barkhamsted, taking in part payment wild timber land in Ohio, and emigrated thence, going by the Erie Canal and lake steamers. For two years after reaching Ohio he lived in the towns of Hiram and Freedom, and then made a settlement in Wellington, Lorain county. He moved his goods with teams, driving his cows, two in number. The roads were new and very muddy, it being in the month of June. They entered the town from the east side, and his land lay in the northeast part, but they were obliged to go five miles around to get one and a half miles. He sent Mary and Pelatiah through the woods with the two cows, as they could get to their destination in a much shorter time than to follow around the traveled road. There was only a narrow footpath through the woods marked by blazed trees, but the distance by this route was only two miles and the boy and girl went alone, picking their way, and came out safe on the opposite side, where they waited several hours for the remainder of their company. The little Mary was twelve years old, and her brother two years younger. They slept on the floor of a neighbor's log house while their own was being built, and this neighbor gave the children some pumpkin pie, which a woman of to-day affirms to be the "best pie she ever tasted."

Two more children were born in Ohio—Albert and Calvin—making a family of eleven children, nine sons and two daughters, to whom I will introduce my readers as my sketch of Matthew Allyn and family progresses. He served five terms in the Connecticut legislature from Barkhamsted. He was a colonel of militia in the war of 1812, and was also justice of the peace and town clerk. It is said of him that he was a "natural scholar." His advantages for schooling were limited, but it was hard to puzzle him on a mathematical problem. He was somewhat eccentric, enjoying jokes in a manner peculiar only to himself. His laugh always came after every one else had ceased laughing, and then he would laugh long and loud.

During the journey from Barkhamsted to Ohio Matthew Allyn took a severe cold which settled in his eyes, and notwithstanding that remedial means were resorted to, the result was for the remainder of his life he was shut in darkness, from all the many beauties which God in his goodness has scattered abundantly on every hand to please the eye and gladden the heart of every child of earth, without regard to rank or station. Thirty years of almost total blindness! Going as a pioneer into the wilds of Ohio, it left great care upon the wife and mother, who heroically placed her shoulder to the wheel, and with the assistance rendered by her brave sons the "wilderness blossomed as the rose."

Matthew Allyn was a great reader, and to be deprived of this blessed privilege was a source of great sorrow, and he labored under a severe nervous prostration; so his children read to him always evenings and all the spare time they could get, which was a source of benefit to them all, as most of his children were remarkably fine readers. He was a man beloved by all who knew him, and was always called Colonel Matthew Allyn. He possessed sterling qualities, high moral principle and a Christian character, which he sustained through many seasons of severe trial. He died January, 1862, aged 68 years.

Clara Merrell, the wife of Matthew Allyn, was considered quite handsome in her girlhood. At that period the ladies when invited to ride by a gentleman were, from the custom and necessity of so doing, obliged to ride either on a blanket or pillion behind their escort. Some were graceful, easy riders; others were timid and would ofttimes fall off. On one occasion there was to be a great party at the Upson house, now known as the 'Squire's house, between Riverton and Pleasant valley. All the young people far and near were invited. Clara Merrell made one of the number, riding behind her beau on a nice blanket of her own workmanship. After leaving Pleasant valley they thought best to whip up the horses and ride across the flat, coming to the Upson mansion in style. The whips were brought into requisition and away went the horses and merry riders. Soon one of the number was missing and one gent found himself without a partner. The horses were brought to a standstill and Clara Merrell was found to have fallen off. An aged lady tells me that whoever invited Clara Merrell to ride horseback was obliged to keep his horse from a canter or else she would change her seat from the saddle to one on the ground in a short time.

It is said of this most noble and worthy Christian woman that "none knew her but to love her." She was for many years a teacher in the Sunday-school, until a short time before her death, and the children for miles knew her and were strongly attached to her. The last time she visited the home of her birth she met the friends of her youthful days, some who, like her, had come from a distance to view once more the familiar scenes of "auld lang syne." The writer of these reminiscences well remembers the days of visiting: the stories that were passed from lip to lip; the merry laugh that followed the recital of each; the songs they sang when life was full of laughter and sunshine, and the yet-unborn future seemed full of promise and brightness; but the voices then were full of the old-time songs of praise and trembled with age, and each one was a prayer as it ascended to the throne of the Great I Am.

Change has visited each one since then. Time's wheel has turned over and over, and carried with it at each revolution some to far western homes; some have passed on into the dark and mysterious portals of Death, while others sit in darkness and sorrow, bereft of home, of friends, and of sight.

Clara Merrell Allyn died in August, 1876. An obituary notice of her death occupied three columns in length in the Wellington *Enterprise;* also a shorter one was presented through the columns of the *Advance*, which will show my readers the love and esteem the people of Wellington and vicinity cherished for her:

"Died at the home of her son, Pelatiah Allyn, in northeast Wellington, September 14, 1876, Mrs. Clara Allyn, widow of Colonel Matthew Allyn, deceased. All knew and loved 'Grandma Allyn.' It is believed that her name is as intimately and necessarily blended with important interests of Wellington as any on the record of its existence.

"Colonel Matthew Allyn and wife with their large family, at a very early day, came from New England and settled in this township, making out of the wilderness the home where the deceased died. Upon the introduction of this family to the then sparse community it was believed that an acquisition of unusual interest was made, and this belief the future proved well founded. Colonel Allyn's character partook largely of liberalized sentiment and personal research, while his wife bore in birth, education, and persistent habits all the sterling qualities of a cultured, conscientious New England lady and matron.

"This family became quite numerous, and their children were spirited and ambitious—all working, useful, and intelligent people, while some compel recognition of unusual merit in literary and business attainments.

"But to return more particularly to a brief notice of the deceased. A word for her is as ample as many, for she lived sacred in the memory of all who have known her. 'Tis said 'Hope springs eternal in the human breast.' With neighbors, friends — everybody — Grandma Allyn's presence increased hope and courage and brought shame to despondency. Purity of purpose, persistency of effort, with effervescing vivacity, were habitual characteristics of a life God had permitted to be of a very great age.

"It may be safely asserted the going out of no other presence in this community could be more sadly missed. Her inspiring enthusiasm and religious zeal have prominently lined this community. The Sabbath-school was with her a great delight and duty; all its interests have been constantly served by her. Duty conquered unusual obstacles, and storms and other inclemencies of weather were never permitted to obstruct her way to her classes. She always had a class.

"Many stalwart men near and far off in the bustle of life will learn of the death of 'Grandma Allyn' with dimmed eyes and quivering lip. Her presence and spirit had made them love the Sabbath-school. Her varied ways had lured to those enchanted places, and religious convictions by her inspired heart blended with unusual love of the teacher and lasting memory of her spiritual power. We loved to meet her always. In her presence the thoughtless were different, the sinning rebuked, the good better. We love to remember her; we love to 'rise up and call her blessed.' She has lived through the lights and shadows of eighty-three years and eleven months, and now her sons and daughters, men and women far down on life's walk, like the people of Wellington, rise up and with one voice call her blessed, blessed mother."

MATTHEW ALLYN'S FAMILY.

Matthew Jr., the oldest son of Matthew and Clara Merrell Allyn, was born February 17, 1817, and in 1836 married Miss Diana Kingsbury. He engaged in mercantile life in Wellington, Ohio, and died in 1851, leaving six children, three sons and three daughters.

The three sons died soon after reaching manhood of that insidious disease, consumption. The two daughters are married. Mrs. Ruth A. Tuttle lives in Chicago; Mrs. Diana Smith in Topeka, Kansas. The oldest daughter married Thomas Ogden, who served in the war and was badly wounded. He afterwards served many years as postmaster in Wellington, Ohio. She died of consumption in Wellington, leaving three children.

Mark Allyn, the second son, was born November 8, 1818. He was of nervous temperament and small in stature. He acquired a classical education—read and practiced law. It is said that a complete biography of the life of this man would make an entertaining and readable volume. He served in the Mexican war, and was a man who had seen much of the world, having made six trips to California by land and water, once via Cape Horn which lasted four months. This was in 1849, and upon reaching California he immediately engaged in mining and accumulated property rapidly. Once in crossing the plains with a train of wagons loaded with merchandise, (two of which were his), they were overpowered by Indians and he with a remnant of the party barely escaped with their lives, leaving everything in the hands of the Indians, with many of their comrades dead on the field. He returned to Ohio in 1855 and married a Miss Young, near the classic shades of Hiram College, presided over by the lamented James A. Garfield. His married life did not prove pleasant. They had one son named Earnest. He moved to Grand Traverse, Michigan, and bought a large tract of land, but his health failed him, and he came in 1873 alone to the old homestead to die among his loved ones.

John Allyn, the third son, has led an eventful life, and as much knowledge of him has been placed at my disposal I propose to devote a chapter to his wanderings.

James Allyn, the fourth son, was born January 1, 1822. He married; and died when but twenty-four years of age in Wellington — his vocation being farming. He left no children.

Mary Allyn, the oldest daughter, was born June 8, 1824. May 13, 1849, she married William H. Saxton, and resides in Oberlin, Ohio. Mary Allyn is of light complexion, dark hair and eyes, and weighs about 180 pounds. She is a genial, pleasant-faced woman of literary tastes, intuitive and original. On one occasion the mother of Mary was heard to say-in reply to the question as to whom she looked like—"I did n't see as she looks like any of the rest, but I can tell you whom she looks like, and that is Betsy Beach, and a real smart-looking girl she was." Mrs. Allyn did not even imagine that she was complimenting her daughter. Betsy Beach used to live down by the Beach Rock, and it derived its name from her father.

Mary Allyn taught school for a number of years. Her husband is by occupation a farmer. They have had five children, four of whom are living: Clara Ardelia, aged 28; married Judson Henry. William John is married and has three children. His age is 26 years. Arthur Albert, aged 20, and Edith May, aged 15. Mary Allyn Saxton lives in Oberlin, Ohio. When she lived in Barkhamsted, a bright-eyed laughing child, she used to attend school where Julia Beecher was the teacher, and now from her Ohio home she sends greetings in her own peculiar manner to her old and still fondly loved teacher, in the following poetical effusion:

> "My dear old teacher I loved so well,
> I loved her more than tongue can tell,
> I loved her then, I love her still,
> I'll now express it with a will."

Julia Beecher used to teach painting in her school, as one branch of education, and Mrs. Saxton has cherished sacredly all these years, the little "cards of merit" with the signature of her teacher and the birds and flowers artistically done in water colors. Mrs. Saxton is quite a poet, and when in conversation with a friend, all unconsciously to herself, she entertains them with specimens of her wit and genius.

Pelatiah Allyn was born May 13, 1826. He is tall, of dark complexion, and weighs about 145 pounds. He was among the early gold-seekers of California. When Mark Allyn left the Mexican war, where he had enlisted for the United States at New Orleans, he went to the gold regions, reaching there with just one dollar in his pocket, but in one or two years had accumulated quite a handsome amount, and on his return home the success he had met with induced his brothers Pelatiah and Phineas, as well as some of his neighbors, to return with him. This was in the year 1851. Pelatiah remained in California two years, and from there wandered to the Australian gold mines, journeying nearly around the globe ere he returned. He lived on the Ohio homestead until 1881, when he sold it, and emigrated to Hardy, Humboldt county, Iowa. He has been a noted hunter, being very expert in killing deer and smaller game. He married in 1863 and has four children.

Phineas Allyn was born September 29, 1829. He is tall, of dark complexion, and weighs about 150 pounds. As before stated, he went to California in 1851 with his brothers and neighbors, and after staying one year returned home with $1,000. He is now located at Duchville, Michigan, and is a prosperous business man, engaged in general merchandising. He acquired a classical education and was a rare linguist. He married Celia Butler in 1854 and had seven children: Celia B., born in 1855, Clara in 1856, Arthur T., 1857, Julia R., in 1860, William Butler in 1863, Nellie in 1865, Watson G., in 1868.

George Allyn, born December 17, 1831, died in 1860, aged 29.

Ann Allyn was born July 15, 1834. She is of dark complexion and medium height. April 14, 1855, she married her cousin, Homer Allyn, who is a prosperous farmer in Wellington. They have six children: Chas. H., born 1856; Mary Sophia, February, 1860; Cora Eveline, March, 1862; Edith Clarinda, January, 1864; Jessie Helen, July, 1871; Hubert Henry, September, 1874. Charles H. is married and has three children, and his vocation, like his father's, is farming. Two of the daughters are graduates and one is a successful teacher.

Albert Allyn was born July 19, 1837. He is of light complexion, tall, and his usual weight is about 140 pounds. He studied law, but in 1881 he removed to Dakota, Aurora county, purchasing three hundred acres of excellent land, which he is improving, and is in most prosperous circumstances. He married in 1861, and is now living with his second wife and has seven children: Grace, born October, 1862; Harry Howard, 1865; Hattie Josephine, 1867; Ethie and Ella, twins, 1870; Abbie Mary, 1877; Bayard Taylor, 1882

Calvin E. Allyn, youngest son of Matthew and Clara Merrell Allyn, was born October 10, 1841. He is 5 feet 11½ inches high and weighs 155 pounds. Is of dark complexion, black hair and eyes; has a dignified, commanding appearance; is affable, courteous, and pleasing in manners; is true, just, charitable, forbearing, trustful, patient, cheerful, and religious—a man of advanced thoughts and progressive ideas. He is a man of fine literary taste and culture, strong powers of mind, and has the love and esteem of the people among whom he resides. July 3, 1861, he married Bina L. Joyce, daughter of Justice Joyce of Wellington, Ohio, before he was twenty years old, his bride being but seventeen, but the war news fired his blood as it had his father's fifty years before, and he enlisted the following September in the 2d Ohio volunteer cavalry, in which he served a little over three years, two years of which was active service in the field in Missouri, Kansas, Arkansas, Indian Territory, Kentucky and Tennessee, he taking part in twenty engagements without harm except gun shots through his clothing. His last year of service was as chief clerk in the Ordnance Department at Headquarters Department of the Ohio, at Knoxville, Tennessee. When his term of service had expired he hastened home to his wife and mother, refusing a salary of $1,200 per year to return, as the ties of home were stronger. His father in 1861 had sent his youngest boy into the face of death with a "God bless you and keep you," and when the son, who had seen his brave comrades fall dead all around him, returned himself unhurt to the home-nest the voice of his father did not reach him welcoming home the wanderer, for in 1862 he had finished the great battle of life and with the ebbing of the tide he had reached the end of the walk from which no wayfarer returns.

In the fall of 1864 Calvin Allyn with his wife, moved to

Cleveland, Ohio, and forming a copartnership with his brother Albert he bought a stock of merchandise and engaged in trade, but sold out again in a few months, when he accepted a position in a lumber yard as salesman, in which business he has been employed since (the last fourteen years as book-keeper), and at present is a silent partner in the firm bearing the name of "Rust, King & Clint."

The wife of Calvin E. Allyn deserves something more than a passing notice. She is a woman who quickly gains the friendship of every one who is brought into the genial atmosphere of her presence. None know her intimately but to love her, she being an intellectual and highly accomplished lady. She is widely known for her charitable and benevolent deeds; is a prominent member of the "Woman's Temperance Missionary Society;" has written and read several papers before the society on the work in China, India, and the Zenana school in Africa, which have been highly complimented. They have had five children. The two oldest died when the little flowers were but mere buds, one little sunbeam removed from their daily life at fifteen months, the other at two years and two months. Ettie E., born July 21, 1865; Nellie A., February 16, 1867; Gertie S., June 3, 1870; Howard E., February 6, 1872, and Ruth M., January 19, 1874. These children are all lovely, are well advanced in school, and Gertie is very proficient in music, playing the piano finely.

JOHN ALLYN,

the third son of Matthew and Clara Merrell Allyn, was born on the ancestral homestead in Barkhamsted, August 29, 1820. As soon as old enough he assisted in the farm work during the summer season, and attended the district school during the winter months. At an early age he exhibited a studious turn of mind, was shy and retiring, and inherited a strong tendency to sick-headache which was so violent as to cause vomiting. He also inherited a feeble constitution, small lungs, which have a tendency to cause the fear of consumption, but by care and temperate habits, regular and moderate activity, he at the present time enjoys uniformly a good degree of vigor and comfortable health.

When he was fifteen years old his father sold the farm in Barkhamsted and moved to Ohio, as before stated, and owing to the great calamity which fell upon the family, in the loss of sight to the husband and father, much labor and responsibility was necessarily thrown upon John, which he met right manfully, realizing that the welfare of the family depended largely upon his exertion. He helped to build a log house, clear a farm, plant an orchard, build and run a saw-mill, and was thus employed until he reached his twentieth birthday. He had an active mind, a retentive memory, was quick to learn, and had been by both father and mother encouraged to cherish the hope that he might acquire a collegiate education. He loved study for its own sake. His thirsty mind was continually reaching out for wisdom and knowledge, but being fully conscious of the inability of his parents to gratify his desire, at the age of twenty his father gave his consent that he should, if possible, educate himself—he to render assistance if it were in his power to do so.

This young man took up bravely the battle, determined to possess the desired prize. He spent two years in Oberlin's preparatory school, supporting himself by working two or three hours a day in summer and teaching in winter. He then went to Quincy, Ill., and continued to pursue his classical studies; read a thorough course of law, was admitted to practice in the supreme court in May, 1846, mostly supporting himself through it all. Not being satisfied with this, he resolved to pursue a course of theological studies, and for that purpose went to Lane Theological Seminary, at Cincinnati.

Before entering this seminary he studied by himself three months, and was fully qualified to enter the second year, and was then permitted to do so, completing the three years' course in a little more than two years, supporting himself in the mean time. At his graduation he was granted the valedictory address, an indication of the highest position in scholarship of the class.

This school at the time was somewhat celebrated, being presided over by Dr. Lyman Beecher; and Professor Stowe, husband of Mrs. H. B. Stowe, of "Uncle Tom's Cabin" fame, was a professor in the same institution. Feeling that he had made great achievements, he did not deem it wise, as he found by this constant labor and close application to study that he had impaired his health. He was then licensed by the Cincinnati Presbytery and entered upon his duties as a Christian minister. He was by nature and training fluent of speech and loved his work, but he found his mind undergoing a change, and a radical one. He d d not consider the theology sound, and passed through a severe mental struggle. He knew he would be misunderstood, his motives suspected, and his chances of advancement and settlement much impaired, but with his conscience upbraiding him he resolved to manfully meet his struggle with duty, and abandon the profession he could not countenance and adorn, and once taking the step he has never looked back upon it with regret.

He then returned to Illinois and taught in the public schools for some time, and next commenced the practice of law in Carrollton. In the fall of 1850 he wrote an essay on the "Will and Moral Nature," which was highly commended by learned men, and he gave it to the public in an attractive form, but it proved too metaphysical to be popular. At this period he suffered for months with debility and various forms of malarial fever.

In the spring of 1851 he went to California by ocean and the isthmus of Panama, going by open boats and mules where DeLesseps is now building the ship canal. He hoped by this change to improve his health and fortune, but had no idea of acquiring great wealth, or of remaining in the country more than a year or two. He took the first ship for San Francisco, which was wrecked and put back for repairs. The next voyage was successful, and he proceeded directly to the mines, which he reached foot-sore, destitute, in feeble health and $400 in debt. Whatever his hands found to do he did it with a will, like thousands of others, without regard to station or education.

When the fall rains came he was obliged to give up mining, not having strength requisite for the severe labor which it involved. He then engaged in making machines for washing gold, at which he secured some capital, which, with his brother Mark as partner, he invested in merchandising in the town of Sonora, where he remained until 1855, when he returned to Illinois and married Miss Sophia Hobson, of Green county, and returned to California.

He had one son, Charles, who is now about twenty-seven years old, and is working in the Star printing-office. This marriage was most unfortunate, and resulted in a separation and divorce. He left all business and went on a mining trip up Frazer river in British Columbia. Not meeting with much success he settled in Victoria and acquired some real estate which soon became valuable. In 1860 he returned east, spent the winter in Ohio, and in the spring he married Miss Sophronia Scott, daughter of the late William Scott, Esq., of Peterboro, N. H., June, 1861, by whom he had twin daughters, both dying. This wife, being an intelligent and thrifty New England woman, proved a blessing and a helpmeet.

At the breaking out of the war they sailed for San Francisco, and on the passage formed the acquaintance of the collector of Puget Sound district, who engaged them to superintend the U. S. Marine Hospital at Port Townsend, W. T. After filling this engagement they passed over to Victoria and made improvement to the property there, but finding the place slow, in 1863 he sold out and removed to Oakland, Cal., where he engaged in real estate, meeting with great success, and in a few years had acquired a handsome competence.

About 1868, when their little daughters were removed by death, the strong winds brought bronchitis to Mr. Allyn, and he was forced to seek a milder climate, which he found in St. Helena, sixty miles north of San Francisco.

During his stay in the east in 1860 he studied dentistry, which he practiced in the Marine Hospital, and afterwards in San Francisco, in connection with his real estate dealings, and now having gained a competence, he is called to-day a rich man at 63 years of age. Within the corporate limits of St. Helena he has purchased twenty acres of fine land, unimproved except a vineyard of twelve acres, which he has cultivated with great success. In 1880 96 tons of grapes grew on it, which sold for $2,400. He built his fine residence, opened an avenue through it and planted a row of eucalyptus trees on each side, some of which are now 18 inches in diameter and 50 feet high.

Mr. Allyn has never sought political life, but served in Sonora as alderman, and in St. Helena as town trustee, and for the past five years as school trustee.

In personal appearance John Allyn is tall and thin, five feet ten inches high and weighs 130 pounds. He is slow in making up his mind in important matters, but of great tenacity of purpose when he reaches a conclusion. Although feeble in physical constitution, he is possessed of great tenacity and reactive force.

This sketch of his life will give my reader sufficient indication of the restlessness of his disposition. From sheer weariness of quiet village life, in 1875 he went to San Francisco to engage in the excitement of mining stocks, where he found even more of this than he had imagined. For six months during the Bonanza excitement he was in the board of brokers every day, and saw fortunes made and lost at every turn of the market. Feeling that this partook too much of the character of gambling, he returned to St. Helena. He depended upon himself and has reached his present attainments and fortune by his own efforts, unaided by capital, or the influence of others. He has attained his ideal of life; has an income sufficient for all his wants and desires. His days are divided thus: Three hours recreative labor in his garden and vineyard, three hours reading and three in writing. At 59 years of age he commenced writing poetry for the press, and some of his poetry has become quite popular in the locality in which he resides.

In concluding this family history, the compiler will add that he does not claim phenomenal talents or achievements for any member of the family; but he does claim that they have been law-abiding, industrious, and self-respecting citizens. He deems the following incident worthy of record: At a family re-union, held at the residence of Homer Allyn, in Wellington, Ohio, in 1880, the oldest representative, in an after-dinner speech, said "that he had never known one bearing the family name to be intoxicated, or to be arraigned before a court for violation of law, or to ask assistance of the public."

PHILOSOPHY

—OF THE—

MIND IN VOLITION.

BY JOHN ALLYN.—PUBLISHED 1851.

CHAPTER I.

WILL DEFINED, AND QUESTION STATED.

1. The question whether will is free or necessitated in its action, is at once the most subtle and comprehensive that ever occupied the human mind. No question has more engaged the thoughts and discussions of philosophers in all ages. And in every age and country within the historic period, the learned and the unlearned, practical men and philosophers, have been nearly equally divided. And yet the idea of the will's action seems to be a key to the science of mind, of morals, an important branch of theology and penal legislation. Important as is this question, and much as it has baffled the investigation of inquiring minds, it is a simple question of facts; the facts are all within and around us, and readily cognizable by the human faculties. After a somewhat patient course of reading and laborious reflection, the whole subject seemed wholly different from the views presented by any writer on the subject.

When most of what follows was first written, not the slightest thought was entertained of its publication in a permanent form; and this was consented to only after earnest solicitations from those whose judgment is considered good in such matters. If the conclusions are sound, they will be useful; if not, let their fallacy be pointed out.

2. For near a century, the *literati* of Europe and America considered the justly celebrated work of President Edwards on the will as unanswerable. Many still think so, while others consider it entirely overthrown. The work is truly great. Such a combination of literary qualities can scarce be found in the compositions of one author, ancient or modern, as is found in Edwards' work. The thought is subtle and penetrating, and at the same time wide-spread, grasping, and exhausting, the reasoning gigantic, and still many of his conclusions

"Like the baseless fabric of a vision."

Some latent fallacy generally lurks in the premises or inferences which vitiates the conclusion.

3. The gist and vital principle of this, as of all other questions, especially abstruse ones, lie in a very small compass. For the sake of brevity, I shall endeavor to confine my discussion to the gist, convinced that those who will not think enough to bring their minds to the "point," will not do so with a tiresome mass of suburb reconnoitering. As an important preliminary to the discussion, the reader's attention is invited to the following

DEFINITION OF WILL.

4. *The will is that power or faculty of the mind by means of which the agent is controlled or controls his own acts and mental states. The will is the mental power or faculty of willing. Willing or volition is an act of mind producing a muscular movement, or a state of mind of similar character, which has not a muscular movement for its object, and in which all the other faculties concur peaceably or forcibly.*

President Edwards' definition of will is not much different. He says: "The will is that by which the mind chooses anything. The faculty of the *will* is that faculty, or power, or principle of the mind by which it is capable of *choosing*. An act of the will is the same as an act of *choosing* or *choice*." *Essay on the Will, page* 2.

Mr. Locke says, "The will signifies nothing but a power

or ability to *prefer* or *choose.*"—*Human Understanding,* 7*th ed., vol. I, page* 197.

5. The attentive reader will observe that in this definition no attempt is made to determine the question whether the will is a distinct organ or faculty of mind, exercising in its acts a given part of the mind, or the whole mind acting in a particular manner or function. It is not the province of the metaphysician to determine which of these is true of volition, or of any thought or feeling. His field is the mind's conscious being and action; and his last appeal is to consciousness, which says nothing of the constituent substance or being of the mind. This is purely a question of phrenology, and must be determined by other methods of investigation. It is generally conceded that every movement of the voluntary muscles is caused by an act of will. But some volitions have nothing to do with the physical, as a willing to suppress a too clamorous desire by awakening pure thoughts and feelings.

I now invite the reader's careful attention to the

STATEMENT OF THE QUESTION.

6. The question is not whether we " do as we please," or whether in the mind's action or volition we are " governed by the strongest motive;" for we have no means of determining the strongest motive, except, as President Edwards says, that it " causes volition." Nor is the question "whether we do as God predetermined we should do." These, and many other issues that have been made, do not reach the merits of the case. This may appear in the sequel.

7. The true question I conceive to be this: Is mind, in its choices, volitions, or actions, governed by, or conformed to, the law of causation, or is it amenable only to the no-law of chance? Is every mental action a link in the great chain of causation? With given antecedents, consisting of the constitution and state of the mind, and all matter outside of the mind that comes in contact with it, so as to exert an influence in the nature of motive, *must* one action, one volition follow, or *may* one or two or more volitions follow? Does the law of causation obtain in the empire of mind as it does in the kingdom of matter? To illustrate—all intelligent persons concede that every particle of matter is moved only as it is acted upon, in accordance with

the laws of matter, which have been reduced to mathematical certainty, in many cases, by philosophers. This is as equally true of the tornado, the volcano, and the cataract, as of the apparently more regular movements of the planets in their orbits.

Take a particle of water as it is condensed from the night air and assumes the globular form in a dewdrop on the petals of a rose; as morning advances it is dispersed, arises in the morning mist, floats off and is mingled with other clouds, is condensed to rain by a shaft of electricity as it flashes across its darkness, falls on the turbid bosom of the Niagara, is hurried over the falls, goes whirling and dashing among the eddies beneath, arises in the spray, floats off to the land, is again condensed, falls, and enters the circulation of a plant, and reappears in nature's paint on the opening petals of its flowers. In all its mutations it moves only as it is moved by the forces acting upon it. With given antecedents, no two motions *can* ensue. In short, every motion of every particle of matter in the universe, is a link in the chain of causation which necessarily connects it back to the Great First Cause, in the impulse imparted to it in the first dawning of creation, with the single exception of miraculous interposition, and such matter as is acted on by mind if the will be free from law.

Now I conceive that the question at issue between the necessitarian and the freedomist resolves itself into this: Is mental action governed by the law of causation? or is every mental action *caused* by an antecedent? I do not recollect of having seen a similar statement by any writer on the subject; but it appears to me, after years of reflection, to comprehend the merits of the case, and to place the subject in a light easier to be understood, and better adapted to discussion than any I have thought of. Therefore I shall discuss the question as stated. I have been thus prolix in the statement, because disputants, in the discussions of abstruse questions, often differ merely because they do not understand each other's positions. I wish to be understood; and have taken thus much pains that those wishing to understand need not *misunderstand* or *misrepresent*. In the next chapter I intend to examine the argument of those who contend for the freedom of the will.

TRUE ISSUE.

8. Since the above statement of the question at issue between the freedomist and necessitarian was in manuscript, it has been pronounced by those whose authority is among the first, a correct and lucid statement of the true issue. But as some whose opinions are entitled to consideration have expressed a doubt of its involving the true issue, it is thought best to add a few considerations, which it was thought unnecessary to embody in the original statement.

The statement of the question, is the will free, is the will necessitated? is too vague for philosophical discussion, until it is determined what it is understood to be free *from*, and what controlled *by*. If we stickle for words, we may get such a succession or concatenation as pleases us, but we can never arrive at clearness of ideas. The word "freedom" in its ordinary meanings, embodies the idea of absence of restraint on our desires or wills; but when applied to the mode of the action of the *will itself*, the meaning must necessarily be somewhat different. It can scarcely amount to a philosophical question whether we are free to do as we please; for though there may be desires in opposition to volition, yet what on the whole pleases us best, we will; and if we are restrained by anything not acting as motive from doing as we will, this has nothing to do with the previous action of the will about which our inquiries appertain. It is not an absurd or impossible supposition that both our *wills* and *our pleasure concerning them*, are controlled in harmony with each other by an irrefragable framework and chain of causation; or they may both act in conformity to absolute contingence, and yet in harmony with each other. To determine which of these is true, we must appeal to "the law and testimony" pertinent to the question.

It can not be a complete issue whether the will acts "spontaneously." The will itself being an active power or principle of the mind, must have greater or less inherent power of acting; and the will in acting cannot be isolated from, but is influenced in the nature of, motive, by the other faculties as they stand extant in consciousness. I confess I do not know what the precise idea is, which is meant to be conveyed by the term "spontaneity of will." Plants are said to grow spontaneously when they are indigenous to the soil and have no assistance from culture; still their growth is according to the law of their own nature. But whether the action of the will be according to its nature, is no question, until it be determined whether that nature and organization for acting, be one of law or contingence.

CHAPTER II.

THE FREEDOMIST'S ARGUMENT EXAMINED.

Man neither does nor can know anything of mind or matter except by observation. —Bacon Transposed.

9. I wish to say in the outset that I entertain sentiments of profound respect towards the authors of whom I speak. Their writings have done the world great service. When I speak of their (supposed) errors, I speak thus positively simply because I think as I say, and do not wish to affect modesty by pretending to doubt.

10. My readers (and especially those unaccustomed to analyze the mental powers and processes) may think there is unnecessary hair-splitting, refinement, and subtlety. To this I answer, it is my province to exhibit the strata, seams, and laminæ of the mental quarry, as the Creator has formed and compacted them. If nature is refined, I must refine; if I succeed in following *her*, I am content.

11. For a long period mankind made very little progress in science, because the method of investigation indicated at the head of this chapter was not pursued; thus the intellect of Greece, Rome, and the middle ages (and there was great power of intellect) was wasted to a great extent in framing systems according to their own notions, instead of investigating how the one we live in is constituted. Since the days of Galileo, Bacon, and Newton, the *investigation* method has been applied, and the progress in physical science has been unparalleled. Although metaphysicians avow this method, I can but attribute the slow progress of mental science to the influence of the old together with the fact that the age has become very practical (if money-

making instead of happiness-seeking is practical); for there is but poor prospect of finding gold in the imperfectly explored caverns of mind; a vein of truth may be discovered, but alas! who will buy it? In Edwards' Essay there is but little of the inductive method, and yet for near a century it was thought impregnable, and is still clung to by many of the older *literati* with the death-grasp.

12. All writers who advocate the freedom of the will, or lawlessness of mind, rely almost solely on the testimony of consciousness for proof of their position. Their other arguments are those deduced from premises which need proof as much as their conclusions. That is their stronghold, their citadel. I shall therefore lay siege to it, for when it is conquered, the whole country is vanquished; if it is impregnable, victory is hopeless. That consciousness is the evidence relied on, Prof. Bledsoe avows in the first paragraph of the last chapter of his book; in which chapter all his argument may be found. President Mahan says (I quote from memory), "when two objects are presented to the mind for choice, we are conscious of power to choose either, and if we choose where there is the stronger motive, we are conscious we had the power to have chosen the other."

13. Now as the whole matter lies coiled up in the word "consciousness," my readers must excuse me for defining the word—analyzing the arguments so confidently deduced from its testimony, and bespeaking their careful attention thereto. Consciousness is the term used by the common consent of writers on mind, to designate the power, faculty, or act of the mind, by which we have knowledge of our own present thoughts, feelings, and volitions, which are the constituent elements of mind. Consciousness gives our mental states as they exist *in præsenti* alone; it goes not into the past except by the aid of memory; it draws no inferences, discovers no laws of action, takes no cognizance of things material or mental, except our own minds. As we observe the form, color, and other qualities of objects by the eye and the observing faculties of the mind, so by consciousness we observe the qualities of our thoughts, emotions, and volitions. By these means we get our facts, or premises. We use the same faculties in reasoning from mental, as from material facts.

14. By this exposition we see that the favorite expression

of President Mahan and other freedomist writers, "we are conscious of power to do a specific act," is compound, loose, unphilosophical, and open to a crowd of fallacies. We are conscious of nothing but a mental state, which may be denominated a feeling of strength! There are two kinds, muscular strength, and mental strength. We will consider the former first. To illustrate, a person using the above phrase says he is conscious of power to lift two hundred pounds or to labor six successive hours in the garden. Consciousness only gives him the present feeling of strength; memory (sometimes treacherous) takes him back to some similar feeling that has existed heretofore, they are compared and pronounced equal. When the former feeling existed, he did lift said weights, and performed said labor. Here are consciousness, memory, comparison, and experience, mixed up and labeled "consciousness" by these metaphysicians.

15. What is denominated a consciousness of power to do a specific act is not a simple "fact of consciousness" which neither needs nor admits of further proof; but is a mere *impression, opinion,* or *judgment,* made up by the complex action of a large number of mental faculties. If opinions are admitted as proof, what cannot be proved? This feeling of strength is by no means a criterion of muscular or mental strength; for this feeling is in the mind, and the strength depends on the state of the muscular and nervous systems, which are material objects not cognizable by consciousness (§ 13), and very variable, but not uniformly so with the feeling of strength. In the above example, with a certain feeling of strength, six successive hours' labor were performed; the person is debilitated by chills and fever—he recovers so as to feel the same feeling of strength, but a short trial will convince him of the imperfection of the test. Mere mental strength is affected by debility of the nervous system in the same way.

16. Further: suppose we have one of several objects to choose; we deliberate, consider, and at length choose. I humbly ask by what principle the freedomist knows that at the time the choice is made it was not prompted by the strongest motive, or, as I prefer to say, was not caused? He answers, "Because I was conscious of power to have chosen the other; and if the first is the stronger and the second the weaker, and I had chosen the second, I should

have chosen where there was the weaker motive, and your chair of causation would have been broken."

17. In addition to the above analysis of "consciousness of power," I answer, that the *strength of motive is the joint product of the state of mind and the objects influencing it* at the time of choice. The external object is no criterion. Five dollars may be a great motive to one man and scarce a motive to another, and a strong motive at one time of life, and scarce a motive at another. The strength of motive that an object excites depends on the state of mind, which is not a fixed fact; it is changeable as the colors of the kaleidoscope. Suppose you had left considering the one you call the stronger and considered the other but for the shortest period of time. This brief consideration may have worked such a change of your mental state as to throw the balance of motive on the object taken, before choice ensued. To illustrate: A man is offered ten dollars as a bribe to do a wrong act; he thinks of the appetites it would afford the means of gratifying; they in turn become excited and clamorous; he is about to accept when he sees his father in the distance; the disgrace he would bring on his family, his own blasted reputation, flash on his mind; the motive has lost its power; he spurns it.

18. Prof. Bledsoe, alone of all freedomist writers, acknowledges that we are not even " conscious of power to act." Prof. Bledsoe's views approximate much nearer to what I humbly conceive to be the truth than those of any other freedomist writer with which I am acquainted. His method of investigation is correct, and he has pursued it much further than his predecessors or contemporaries, but stopped short of what appears to be the whole truth.

19. Presuming that my motives will not be misconstrued, I will venture the following opinion that he was led to error as thousands have been before. It became thoroughly grounded in his mind that his own or his opponent's opinion was correct; he pored over it till he *saw* there was no foundation for that of his opponent. With all the rejoicing of the victor he jumped to the conclusion that his own was true. Had he scanned his own position as closely as he did that of his adversary, perhaps he would have seen, what I think will appear in the sequel, that there was no truth in either.

20. He says (page 226): "By consciousness, then, we dis-

cover the existence of an act. We see no cause by which it is produced. If it were produced by an act or operation of anything else, it would be a passive impression, and not an act of the mind itself. The mind would be wholly passive in relation to it, and it would not be an act at all. Whether it is produced by a preceding act of the mind or by the action of anything else, the mind would be passive as to the effect produced. But we see in the clear and unquestionable light of consciousness that instead of being passive the mind is active in its volitions; hence it follows by an inference as clear as noonday and as irresistible as fate that the action of the mind is not a produced effect."

21. Here he rests his cause. We are conscious the mind acts; this I grant. This is an *act*, not an impression; if it were *caused*, it would be an impression, not an act. As the argument of the whole book is converged to a focus at this point, let us examine it with care. This conclusion is what logicians call a *non sequitur*. The minor premise, that volition is an act, is true; the inference, therefore, that it is not caused does not necessarily follow. The state of the mind is always included in every legitimate estimate of motive (§ 17); if, then, this, including its active nature and its excitants in the external world, are a "ground and reason why it acts as it does rather than otherwise," they constitute a cause. By what philosophy is this determined or deduced from the fact that the mind acts? Consciousness gives the present mental states and acts; nothing more, not even the *laws* of mental action. The mind is active in volitions, but is there an absurdity in the idea that motive causes it to act, or to act as it does rather than otherwise?

22. Prof. Bledsoe says (page 216): "No one ever imagined that there are no indispensable antecedents to choice, without which it could not take place." These "antecedents" are in part always motives external to the mind, of which consciousness can take no note. By what principle, then, can it be known that these objects do not sustain such a relation to the mind as to constitute what is termed the strongest motive or a *cause* of the subsequent *action?* Can this be done without even an examination of these objects? He acknowledges that there must be an antecedent, but does not examine it. He disposes of it summarily by saying it is not caused because it is *active*.

23. When a ball is thrown against an elastic substance it acts; it is active as well as passive. Is Prof. Bledsoe conscious that when the mind acts it does not act in accordance with the laws of mind as acted on by these "indispensable antecedents," which are out of sight, to occasion them to act.?

24. The germination of seeds affords a good analogy to mental action. The seed acts—that is, there is action among the constituent particles of matter—and the germ shoots forth; there are also some "indispensable antecedents" to its action. There must be warmth and moisture. So, when a needle is attracted by a loadstone, it (the needle) acts or moves. Suppose the seed and the needle were endowed with consciousness, they might proudly say, "True, we cannot act without antecedents; but then our movement is an act, not an impression; therefore, by an 'inference clear as noonday and irresistible as fate' we are free from law. Your chain of causation is broken; it has no power over *us*." I present these physical cases as illustrations, not proofs.

25. The truth seems to be we are conscious the mind acts; whether it acts in accordance to the laws of mind can only be determined by observing whether there is a similarity or diversity of subsequent acts after similar antecedents. In the next chapter an original investigation will be presented, when I think the above views will be clearer than now.

CHAPTER III.

ORIGINAL INVESTIGATION OF THE MODE OF MENTAL ACTION IN VOLITION.

26. I have now arrived at the proper point, to present the only legitimate mode of investigating this subject, by applying the Baconian or inductive method, and the results of such investigation. The question is, Does mind always act in accordance with law, the antecedent being such as to *cause* the volition?

27. These antecedents consist of the mental states and all the matter that is so related to it as to influence it in the

nature of motive, at the time of volition (§ 17.) This material motive consists of the objects of choice external to the mind, and all that organized matter, which (so to speak) borders on and surrounds mind, consisting mainly of the nervous system, through which mind acts and is acted upon. The quality and condition of this latter so varies the influence of the former, that all calculations that do not take this into the account are uncertain. A sum of money is offered a person if he will commit perjury; while he thought of the appetites it would gratify, the wants it would supply—he is strongly inclined, or even resolved, to accept; but with no variation of anything external to the mind, by its own action he considers the wrong it would do to some one, the danger and disgrace of detection, and the power of the motive is materially changed. So suppose the mental state be fixed, and let the bribe be increased from a hundred to a thousand dollars, and possibly he might accept. And let both remain fixed, and the nervous system changed (were it possible) from a healthy to a morbid tone, and no sagacity can predict the result. Therefore the power to produce volition or strength of motive, is the joint product or offspring of the state of mind, and all external objects influencing it.

28. The question being whether the antecedents being equal, the volitions are always the same, it can only be determined by observing the antecedents when equal, and the subsequent volition. With equal antecedents, if one case of diverse volitions can be found, the question is settled; the freedomists are right—the will is free from law. But if no such case can be found, there is no proof of freedom; but how many cases of equal antecedents and consequents are necessary to evoke a principle, my readers may judge for themselves. The difficulties of the investigation are now sufficiently apparent. As a part of the antecedent is the state of the mind at the time of volition, it is utterly impossible to ascertain that of another with sufficient accuracy for philosophical experiment, by its external manifestation. Every one must use himself to experiment with; and it may be fairly doubted, considering the almost infinite complication of the mental faculties, whether the same antecedents ever occur twice in the same person, much more a sufficient number of times to establish a principle. But waiving this, in making the observation the

whole mental state must be grasped by consciousness, and held firmly in the memory; for the least play of fancy may vary the result. At the same time the whole field of matter influencing the mind, including the state of the nervous system, must be grasped by the observing faculties, and the volition observed. This process is a pattern, and must all *in minutiæ* be held in memory. The process of observation and comparison must be carried on till another equivalent state of antecedent is found, and the volition observed. This counts one. This must be repeated times enough to establish a principle. I confess that it appears such an investigation would require a strength and a stretch of the intellect beyond the power of any living man; and yet it appears to be the only direct method, reasoning from cause to effect, of settling this vexed question. There is sufficient circumstantial evidence in favor of the legality of mental action, to raise *prima facie* evidence. This will be considered in the next chapter, and if it is made out, the case must stand adjudged to the law side, till it is rebutted.

CHAPTER IV.

CIRCUMSTANTIAL EVIDENCE.

29. Although the direct investigation of this abstruse subject seems so fruitless, there is some circumstantial evidence which deserves attention. The first I shall consider is the argument from analogy. It is one of the first elements of Natural Philosophy, and the ground of philosophizing, that every particle of matter moves, or is moved, in conformity to the laws of matter. This is and has been the case throughout the entire realm of the material universe, with no exception but miraculous interposition. That *law* prevails through one part of the same Creator's dominions, seems to raise an analogy that it does in all departments. But this is far from being conclusive. Analogy never *proves* anything. Besides, the nature and operation of mind is so different from that of matter, that the force of the analogy is very much weakened. This is the sum total of President Edwards' argument of cause and

effect. He says, "volition is an effect; every effect must have its cause; and that cause must be motive." But in assuming, as he did, without an attempt at proof, that volition is an effect, he begged the whole question.

30. We will now array the circumstantial evidence. Since the state of mind and external objects influencing it, or motives, are the antecedents to volition, if the law of causation be abrogated, and they have no causative power, it irresistibly follows that it is impossible to form a judgment or even a probable guess what the volition will be from the antecedents. The action of the will is the merest chance; though motives are piled like

"Alps on Alps and Pyrenees beyond,"

choice is just as likely to be in an opposite direction where there is no motive at all except as an object of choice, as where there is the greatest possible accumulation. All the means we have of judging future conduct is by observing mental and material facts and relying on the principle that like antecedents produce like subsequents. But if this principle fails in mind we can form no idea of future mental action in any case.

31. The infinite mind of Deity might *know* how mind would act, for by the hypothesis of infinity, the past, the present, and the future are all present, and that independent of the procuring cause of the event. But *we* who must climb to future events on the ladder of causation, will at once come to the ground if causation fails. Now, is this true in mental action? It is either true in whole, or true in part, or not true at all. Common observation teaches that it is not true in whole. We know that "human nature" is a matter of study, or science to some extent. Those who are shrewd, knowing the facts influencing the mind, can tell with almost prophetic certainty how a person or a community will act. And the more accurately they know the external circumstances, and the disposition, or mental state of the person, the greater is their certainty. And further, when men fail, they always attribute it to a mistake or ignorance of some influence or disposition, and not to a failure of the law of causation. These facts prove, being inconsistent with any other hypothesis, that the law of causation prevails to some extent, but with all these facts it is

possible that within a limited sphere the will is free, and its action a matter of chance. But I profess the above facts present a bulwark of *prima facie* evidence which cannot be rebutted by any argument I have thought of or seen.

CONCLUSION.

32. Reader, my task (and yours if you have followed me through) is done. I might have extended and expanded this essay to a much greater bulk with even less labor. But I wished to study all the brevity consistent with perspicuity. When I began I had no creed to support; now I have done I have no inferences to draw. I endeavored to divest myself of all predilections and preconceptions, and address myself to "nature as the humble interpreter thereof." I have something to say with regard to the bearings of this essay on ethics, or theoretical and practical morality; but I think best to withhold it for the present till my thoughts are more mature and an opportunity shall be presented which premises good. With entire unconcern this essay is submitted to a candid public; if it is error, let it perish; if truth, it will prevail.

CHAPTER V.

RELATIONS OF THIS ESSAY TO FATALISM AND EXERTION.

33. The doctrine of the foregoing essay is often supposed to be connected with a paralyzing, ruinous fatalism. Indolence and immorality argue, that if all phenomena, both physical and mental, are bound up in the iron chain of causation, and the first part actually transpired, effort on my part is useless, for things will have their course. However groundless this may be, there is a sufficient plausibility in it to deserve a careful consideration.

34. Modern metaphysicians have agreed in dividing the mind into three great departments; the intellect, the sensibility, and the will; and if they had not, the reader could, for his own convenience. The intellect is the perceiving, knowing department; the sensibility, the department of emotions and desires; the will, the department of volition.

Now, in all classes of exertion to acquire a supposed good, the following process must take place: First, the intellect sees a supposed good, the desire is awakened to obtain it, the will puts forth volitions, and a thousand muscles stand, like dumb slaves about a prince, to put its mandates in execution. Then comes the feeling of exertion or fatigue, which is nothing more than a feeling of the mind consequent on a state of the muscles, caused by their vigorous contraction and relaxation. Now, as the action of the muscles is always after volition, and the question between freedomists and others is whether the relation between the sensibility and the will be one of law or chance, it will be seen, in either case, that in obtaining the desired good, exertion and fatigue is equally a concomitant. Mere mental exertion and fatigue, or exertion of will, are of the same nature; its fatigue being caused by the matter of the nervous system. To make exertion without perceiving what it is for, is to immerse man in darkness; and if we can make exertion without willing to do so, "we might as well not have a will." As exertion and fatigue are the only unpleasant parts of the process intervening between us and a desired object, the mind is occupied by these unpleasant parts, and the other acts of the mind are overlooked; hence the error. If we desire the accomplishment of anything, it will be done if we make the necessary exertion (for exertion cannot take place without the other parts of the mental process). And as before observed, that exertion and fatigue are the same concomitants of the acquisition, whether the will act legally or not; and as exertion and fatigue come after volition, the only difference is this: that if the object be self-improvement by awakening the mind, by thought, or reading, the object when obtained becomes in turn a motive. Now if the will is governed by causation it *must* act, and thus successive rounds take place; but if the will is free the whole may stop with the first object. So if the will be free from law, the preacher or lecturer may ply his most powerful arguments with all the talents of an angel, literally inflaming the emotive part of the mind; but it is all to no purpose; the will is no more likely to act than if no motive were before it. But if law govern the will, like seed sown on well-prepared soil, it *must* produce its legitimate effects, unless counteracted by an intervening line of causation. Some say, "I do as I please, therefore I am free." When we *will*, or *act*, notwithstanding there are strong motives to the contrary, we always do on the whole as we please. This phrase means that we are not interrupted by any thing *ab extra*, nothing more.

35. The vulgar frequently excuse themselves, when reproved for doing what they know is wrong, by saying it was so fated. If you have done the deed, you are, like Zeno's slave, fated to receive the consequent punishment; which if you are wise you will recollect as a motive to prevent doing the like again. If you have not done the deed, you will so consider the reproof that it will become a motive, to save you from the fated deed and fated punishment; "but fools pass on and are punished."

36. I do not conceive that this question affects the theological one of predestination at all; for if Deity be infinite in knowledge He must know the beginning, middle, and end of all things equally, whether law or chance reign; and I have not acumen enough to separate between foreknowledge and predestination, that is, to see how one can exist and the other not. But whether God does or does not know and predestinate our end, makes not a particle of difference; for our state at every successive step and movement to all eternity would be known and certain if there was a being who had sagacity enough to foresee them, whether law or chance reign. But our inquiries must relate to human minds and those things and events that surround them, and not to those of a higher grade. It is a question of fact; and philosophy here, as ever, coincides with common sense; if we desire any object, nothing intervenes that need trouble us, but the exertion requisite to its obtention; if we prefer our ease, we can have it.

CHAPTER VI.

ORIGINAL SUGGESTION CONSIDERED.

37. The foregoing essay has been read in manuscript by a gentleman who sustains a high reputation as a teacher of mental science, and has for years presided over a popular western college. He has politely furnished me with an abstract of his views of the doctrine advanced. He thinks

the question correctly stated, and successfully overthrown as stated by freedomists; still he thinks the doctrine of the freedomist can be sustained. His statement is, that "we are so made that, at each instant up to the final act of choice we cannot but assume that we are free to choose either the one or the other. It is rather an original suggestion than a consciousness. The mind always does believe, and *must* believe, itself adequate, all existing causation to the contrary notwithstanding, to choose either the one or the other. My argument for the freedom of the will is, that such an original suggestion never deceives; that what mankind are so made as necessarily to think true, and to act on as true, is true."

38. No other definition is given to the term "original suggestion" than can be gathered from the above statement. Mr. Upham says the term is used by Reed, Stuart, and others, to express the simple fact "that the mind by its own activity and vigor, gives rise to certain thoughts," and "by means of this we have a knowledge of certain elementary notions, such as the abstract conception of existence, mind, self-existence, or self, personal identity, succession, duration, space, unity, number, power, right, wrong, and some others. All men possess these notions; all understand them."

39. That there is a power of the mind to give us these notions (by whatever name you call it) may be admitted; but it is an open question whether the freedom of the will from the law of causation is an original or an artificial suggestion. It is conceded that all human beings either have, or all have not this faculty; if they have it, some will have it in greater perfection than others. All writers on mind agree that this faculty suggests the same truths to all minds not of too low a grade for its distinct action; certainly there is no contradiction. If it gives one man self-existence, it does all men; if it gives one man duration, space, and their infinity, it does all men. In matters of opinion, reasoning, and judgment, men differ, on account of the complexity of the mental processes by which these states of mind are elaborated. But notions of suggestion, coming from the fountain of the mind, or being the result of a simple action of a simple power or faculty of the mind, *must* be true, or all reasonings and knowledge are at an end; for the premises of all reasonings are obtained in this way, as well as

inference itself. If the primary action of the mental faculties is to be questioned, pray what is the criterion of truth? Are we to refer to angels? Now let us try this idea of causeless volition by some of the above tests.

40. Is it a primary idea, thrown out by the inherent energy of all minds sufficiently developed? If so it would be the same in all men. So far from this, men are, and always have been, nearly equally divided on the question. In 1848, American missionaries, in Asia Minor, wrote that the Mahometan inhabitants believed in fatality and "*acted on it as true;*" that when the cholera was sweeping off appalling numbers, they would not go to the country from the overcrowded city, or make any exertion to avert any evil, on the ground of fatality. I suppose that all the followers of Mahomet, about one half as many as those of Christ, believe in the causation of volition, "and act on it as true." If it be said that "these were uncultivated minds," I answer, that Edwards, Emmons, and a large and respectable religious denomination have believed, and still believe, in it. If our friends would have us believe that the mind originally suggests that volition is not caused, it devolves on them to show how so many came by an opposite idea, or belief. In the mean time we will undertake to account for the idea of freedom otherwise than by suggestion.

41. The mass of mankind have not, even in our own country, thought of the subject enough to have a distinct idea of the question at issue. The uncertainty as to how the mind will be determined—the power of deliberation—and the freedom from restraint or constraint, have led many to suppose they were free; indeed, this is the very idea of freedom with many. But all of this is perfectly consistent with the idea of causation in volition. The *iron* jacket sits as easily on our *mind* as the vast weight of the atmosphere on our *heads*. Thus we apprehend that multitudes adopt the sentiment of freedom from mere *mental crudity*. Mahometans adopt the opposite idea from the same cause; the opinions of both are equally worthless, except it be to show that original suggestion is silent on the subject.

42. That part of freedomists which cannot plead crudity, we venture to presume, have some favorite doctrine of theology or morals, which they suppose inconsistent with caused volition. Their cherished doctrine is not doubted, so they, unconsciously, seek for arguments against caused volition.

43. A friend of the writer, of great metaphysical acumen, after reading the forgoing essay, acknowledged that causation prevailed in all volitions except those constituting moral acts, or actions right or wrong. His argument was about this: Men are under moral obligation to do and refrain from certain acts; this obligation is often violated; if volition is caused, they *could not* have done otherwise (if they had tried), and what men cannot do they are under no obligation to do. To say they could not have done otherwise if they had tried, is absurd. Effort and volition always coincide, except constrained by some force *ab extra*. I will not dissect this argument further now, but state it here because what is to follow will apply to *it* as well as to the foregoing argument.

44. If it can be shown that the hypothesis of freedom is inconsistent with known and acknowledged facts or principles, or involves absurdity, it must be given up. Chance and contingence are words used in two senses. First when the causes of phenomena are so complicated or hidden that they cannot be traced. Thus we say it is a chance if it rains; when dice are shaken and thrown, it is a chance how they will fall; when a coin is thrown up with a whirling motion, it is contingent which side up it will fall. But no one supposes that the law of causation fails in any of these cases. Second, these words are applied to describe uncaused phenomena; volitions on the hypothesis of freedom are the only examples of these.

45. Even these events (if freedomists are right) are equally certain as any event whatever, only *our* means of ascertaining that certainty do not exist. But God, if He be omniscient, and perhaps inferior beings, can see what, or how, these absolutely contingent phenomena will be, which proves them to be certain in an absolute sense. All that is meant by the first definition is obscurity of causes; by the second, absence of causes.

46. Now within the sphere of freedom, that is, with regard to those objects of which the mind is supposed to be free to choose either, it is a matter of absolute contingence which will be taken; for the very hypothesis of freedom is uncaused volition; and all the necessary *occasions* of choice are a choosing subject, and an object of choice.

47. All the writers on mind agree that all the actions of the intellect and sensibility are governed by causation;

4

therefore a given state of mind and given external objects will produce always the same excitation of intellect and sensibility.

48. Now if mind is self-determined, or self-acting, regardless of causation, it is one of two things— self-determination of person, or self-determination of will. If it be self-determination of person, as the person includes both the intellect and sensibility, and as their excitation are the only immediate motives to the will, if it is determined according to the paramount excitation of them, it is according to causation. But if the person wills contrary to his paramount inclination, it is absurd. But if the will is self-determined, then the will leads the person by the nose, and the will is led by this little inane personage called chance, who struts in his "brief hour of authority," and pays not the slightest regard to the wishes, desires, or even the moral sense of the person.

49. On the hypothesis of freedom, within the sphere of freedom, there can be no means of *judging* or *guessing* what volitions will be; nor from past volitions, what the disposition of mind *was*. All means are swept away, and there can be no such thing as habitude or character; each volition is individual, isolated, uncaused, not affected by antecedents. How then does one action afford any clue to what the next action will be? It is not easy to see how, on the hypothesis of freedom, such a thing as habitude or character can exist. By the hypothesis, between the volitions and the mental excitations, either of the sensibility or intellect, which alone primarily influence the will as motive, there is a gulf as impassable as that between Dives and Lazarus. I confess I cannot see how one act can influence a succeeding one, to be morally good or bad, except that the first act and the mental excitation accompanying it, and causing it (if it is caused), by a law of our nature, produce a habitude of the thoughts and feelings antecedent to the subsequent act. But how can this be, since by the hypothesis of freedom the act is uncaused, totally isolated from all antecedent motives, and absolutely contingent? How then can character or habitude good or bad exist? Yet they do exist.

50. It is equally difficult to see what is gained to the cause of morals by cutting off all connection between the volitions and the moral feelings; if the moral act be caused,

it is an outward expression of the internal man; if not, it is an illegitimate intruder into the world, both dumb and blind, and can neither tell the moral feelings, thoughts, intentions, or succeeding acts. To be subject to law, and have one's moral acts the sport of fancy, would seem hard, but to be controlled by chance is worse; for fancy has some regard to law, chance none.

51. If they be caused, the pain of punishment adds another motive to those, the office of which is to cause the person to do right. But if they are uncaused, their punishment is wanton vengeance, in every possible respect. Men are led into error by reasoning that it is unjust to punish a man for doing what he could not help doing if he tried. Here are two errors; first, that punishment is a vengeance and a hardship to the guilty; it is for *their* good, as well as for the good of others. Second, that one ever really *tries* contrary to causation or volition.

52. Should it be said, " if you know a man's main object, you may foresee the particular volition he will put forth in its execution," I answer, most freedomists allow that when a man's main purpose is formed, all minor volitions in execution thereof are caused; as when I set out to walk to a town five miles distant, the several volitions which move my legs are considered necessary. One's " main object " is changed but a few times in one's life; and it matters but little whether these volitions are caused or uncaused, if they are the only uncaused ones. I can see no other force to the above quoted reasoning, than to narrow the sphere of freedom, but when you come to that sphere (by which term I include all those volitions which the mind is supposed to be free to make either) the above reasoning must apply. It is not my province to define that sphere, since I believe in none; and freedomists themselves differ as to what it includes, all agreeing that some volitions are caused. I am content if I so frame my argument that it will apply to all that *are* included, be they more or less.

53. If it be said that " the preceding act, or the mental excitation accompanying it, exert an influence on a succeeding one, though not a causative one," I answer, it does not appear how antecedents can, " in whole or in part, be a ground or reason why a volition is, rather than not, or why it is as it is, rather than otherwise," and not cause it. It should be borne in mind that we have no measure of mo-

tive as an external object, and it matters not whether it influence the will much or little; if it affect the will at all it must be a causative effection, or a contingent effection. In the latter case, with given antecedents, the volition is contingent, to which all the forementioned appurtenances attach.

PART II.

REVIEW OF EDWARDS ON THE WILL.

CONSISTING OF A CANDID STATEMENT OF HIS SEVERAL POSITIONS AND ARGUMENTS; AND THEIR CAREFUL EXAMINATION.

CHAPTER I.

54. Part first is merely an attempt to define all the terms of uncertain import, used in the following discussion. In Section first the will is defined to be *"that by which* the mind chooses any thing: the faculty of the will is that faculty, or power, or principle of the mind, by which it is capable of choosing:" this is variously illustrated, and some criticisms made on some observations of John Locke on the subject.

55. Section second consists of an inquiry as to "what determines the will." He says, *"it is that motive which, as it stands in the view of the mind, is the strongest, that determines the will,"* I suppose he means, *at the time of volition.* He then goes on to explain what he means by *motive;* which is "the whole of that which moves, excites, or invites the mind to volition, whether that be one thing singly, or many things conjointly." In further elucidating the matter he says, "a motive has some sort and degree of tendency, or advantage to move or excite the will previous to the effect, or to the act of will excited. This previous tendency is what I call the strength of motive." Here we have the two distinct measures of the strength of motive, more

variant than avoirdupois and troy weight, and wine measure! The first example is another example of *petitio principii*, or begging the question. If the will is moved, as he contends, by an antecedent cause, and its action necessitated, then that which determines, or is the cause of the will's action, is the strongest or greatest. But if the will is free, and acts spontaneously and contingently, then the motive which is before the mind and is the *occasion* of its acts may not be the strongest or greatest. The president's assertion, that the former is true, though high authority, will hardly be taken in this investigating age, in lieu of all evidence of the fact.

56. The second proposition is clearly erroneous, as it will appear hereafter. But the whole difficulty consists in the absurd attempt to apply a measure to motive, considered as by him, as something external to the mind, that "moves, excites, or invites the mind to volition." In the first proposition he says, "that motive is the strongest which, as it stands in the view of the mind, determines the will." Suppose this *dictum* is true, what does it avail as a measure of the strength of motive, when there is no probability, and scarce a possibility, of its ever standing in the same view of the mind a second time? Mind is ever active, and the slightest variation of the excitement of any of the faculties, when it views the motive, must change the strength of the motive. And further if the same motive should ever a second time "stand in the same view of the mind," he has offered no evidence that volition would be the same: if the doctrine of the freedomist is true, there is no probability that it would. His second measure of the strength of motive is, its previous tendency to excite or move the will? A bottle of rum may have a previous tendency to excite a man whose appetite is morbid and excited, to commit theft; but a moment's *reflection* may so bring before his mind the shame and disgrace he is bringing on his family, as to counteract the "previous tendency." If he had added to his previous tendency, with a given view, state, or excitement of mind, it would have been correct; but of what avail? Motive, properly speaking, can only be measured by estimating both the mental excitement, and all external matter influencing it, at the time of admeasurement.

57. Section 2d contains a definition of philosophical or metaphysical necessity; which is "nothing different from

their certainty. Not certainty of knowledge, but the certainty of things themselves, which is the foundation of the certainty of the knowledge of them, or that wherein lies the ground of the infallibility of the proposition that affirms them." And again, "philosophical necessity is really nothing else than the full and fixed connection between the things signified by the subject and predicate of a proposition."

58. In Section 4th, the distinction between natural and moral necessity is said to be "not so much in the connection as the terms connected." In natural necessity the terms are material, in moral, the terms are moral or rather metaphysical. These definitions are variously explained and illustrated, and the difference between their philosophical and popular use pointed out. Would it not conduce to clearness to say material and mental necessity, as this is the "idea"?

59. Section 5th contains a definition of liberty and moral agency. The popular sense of liberty is, the freedom from re-straint or con-straint from doing or acting as we please or will. But the liberty which "Arminians advocate and Calvinists deny is a self-determining power of the will by which it determines its own volitions; without being affected by any cause out of itself, or prior to its own acts specified. Also indifference must belong to it, or that the mind previous to the act of volition be *in equilibrio*. Absolute contingence also belongs to it" (and I may add that this is all the absolute contingence in the universe, and if the will is not thus free, there is no absolute contingence). Leaving the subject of the will, and entering the field of ethics, some good remarks as to moral agents, and moral character, close the section.

60. Having closed the definitions in part first, in part second he argues the case. In Section 1st, he examines what he calls the "Arminian notion of liberty of will, consisting of the will's self-determining power." He employs the *ad absurdum* argument, by saying that if the will, or, as he prefers it, the agent or person willing, determines its or his own acts, it must be by a previous act of will, and that previous act by another preceding act, and so on *ad infinitum*, or to the first act in the series, which must be, he says, caused by something else.

61. I confess I am not able to see the force of this argu-

ment. I suppose the "Arminian notion" to be, that the will, or person, determines its own acts, by its own inherent energy or action, aside from external or even internal influence in the nature of motive, *when it acts and in the act of acting*. Is there anything inconsistent or absurd in the idea? It is a question of fact, and should be treated as such by examining the evidence in the case. To say that it is, or must be determined by a preceding act is simply to beg the question; and further when he comes to the first act in the series, it is mere assumption to say it is not a free act. He seems to have it fixed in his mind that volition *must* have a cause. The hypothesis of freedom is that it is not (so to speak) enticed by something before it, to cause it, in the shape of motive; nor driven by something (a previous act), with whip in hand behind it; the whole begins and ends in assumptions and proves nothing.

62. Section 2d contains a consideration of some evasions of the argument of Section 1st. When the foregoing comment on Section 1st was written, I had not read Section 2d, nor had I any idea of what it contained. But on its careful perusal I do not see that anything can be said to throw light on the subject, nor do I see cause to change what has been written on Section 1st.

63. Section 3d purports to be an inquiry " whether any event whatever, and volition in particular, can come to pass without a cause." He defines cause " to signify any antecedent, either natural or moral, positive or negative, on which any event, either a thing or the manner and circumstances of a thing, so depend that it is the ground and reason, either in whole or in part, why it is rather than not, or why it is as it is rather than otherwise." He then says, "Having thus explained what I mean by cause, I assert that nothing ever comes to pass without a cause. And this dictate of common sense respects substances and modes or things and the manner and circumstance of things." He then goes on to being and mode of being of *bodies* as universally referred to cause. I will quote one passage, not that it contains a pertinent argument, but on account of its intrinsic worth:

64. " If once it should be allowed that things may come to pass without a cause, we should not only have no proof of the being of a God, but we should be without evidence of the existence of anything whatever but our own immediate

ideas and consciousness; for we have no way of proving anything else but by arguing from effect to cause; from the ideas immediately in view we argue other things not immediately in view; from sensations now in the mind we argue things without as the causes of these sensations; we argue the past existence of ourselves or anything else by memory only as we argue that the ideas which are now in our minds are the consequences of past ideas and sensations; we immediately perceive nothing else but the ideas that are this moment extant in our minds; we perceive or know other things only by *means* of these, as necessarily connected with others and dependent on them; but if things may be without causes, all this necessary connection and dependence is dissolved, and so all means of our knowledge is gone." This is a magnificent and beautiful passage, but does not reach the point. It may be unfortunate to "have no proof of the being of a God," but still it is difficult to see how this can be wrought into an argument that *mind* does not so act. It seems unnecessary to examine the assumptions of this section further.

65. Section 4th inquires whether *volition* can arise without a cause, through the activity of the nature of the soul. The mere activity of the soul neither proves nor disproves that the action of that activity is or is not in accordance with the law of causation. Animals and plants are to some extent active in their nature; but I suppose that all acknowledge that their movements are all caused. The issue is, are all the particles (so to speak) or constituent elements of the substance or being of the soul in the process of volition in conformity to the law of causation? The question is one of fact, and all this declamation about the law of cause and effect in matter, or even in the emotive or intellectual part of our nature, is not evidence pertinent to the issue.

66. It is not easy to see the force of the *ad absurdum* argument in the fifth paragraph which he attempts to father on his opponents. It is of a similar nature to his argument in reference to a self-determining power of the will. In the present case the hypothesis is that the soul chooses or acts freely, or in violation of the law of causation, as it exists from the presence of motive, through the inherent activity of the soul, *when it chooses, or in the act of volition*. Now, to undertake to prove this untrue by saying that if the will

act freely it must be by a previous act of choice, is nothing more than an assumption. I mean no disrespect, or that the author meant to befog himself or his readers, but it seems that such is the case. He says, "he cannot conceive what is meant by the soul's choosing by its own activity, except that God has given power to the soul, sometimes, at least, to excite volitions at pleasure or according as it chooses; and this certainly supposes in all cases a choice preceding all volitions which are thus caused." I fear I shall weary the reader by repetitions; but this does seem to be an evasion of the true issue as stated above.

67. In Section 5th, his remarks on Dr. Whitbey's idea of liberty as a power of acting from ourselves, or doing what we will, are very just; but as that *idea* is not the *true idea*, but little is gained or lost to either cause by its refutation.

68. Section 6th contains a consideration of the idea of choosing things which are indifferent. The position of Dr. Whitbey is fully met and refuted. The position taken by Dr Whitbey is this: When two things are presented to the mind which in the view of the mind have equal claims to choice, if one be chosen it proves liberty of will. It is a sufficient answer to this, that, although the motive in each object is equal, yet in the moment of, and in the act of choice, the motive to choose one is superadded to the motive in the object. It is scarcely necessary to observe here that this overthrowing of these false issues does not affect the true issue.

68. Section 7th is a further consideration of the liberty of will consisting in indifference. I cannot but protest here that I am tired of commenting on arguments which, on both sides, are founded on assumptions instead of facts. Much is said and some fine-spun arguments deduced, but no headway made.

69. I protest further, that in writing this review I have no ambition to vanquish the writer reviewed. It is no great honor to cut off a dead lion's head, should the undertaking prove successful. It would be much more congenial to my feelings, avoiding controversy, to rest the cause with presenting my own views; but I judged that the reputation of President Edwards' work has been, and still is, such as to demand a review from any one who attempts a complete exposition of the subject. As I advocate substantially the same conclusions as President Edwards, it may seem un-

necessary to write, and an anomaly to review the writer. A president of one of our colleges remarked to me that he "thought Edwards would no longer satisfy the demands of a thinking age." Although I think his conclusions true, yet I think he has loosely and bunglingly proved them, if at all; for these and other reasons I write a review.

70. So, with again bespeaking the reader's patience, I will again to my task. The idea he is combating, as far as I can translate it, is this: that when the mind is in *equilibrio*, or perfectly indifferent which of two objects to choose, and by the exertion of the inherent powers of the will, aside from all influence on it in the nature of motive, one is chosen, this is a free, uncaused act. His (that is, Edwards') argument is, that to constitute it a free act the mind must be *in equilibrio*, not only before, but in the act of choice, which he correctly says is absurd!

71. Section 8th is a consideration of liberty of will, as opposed to all necessity. All that need be said on this point is that the whole point in controversy is assumed by the argument that all things in general, and volition in particular, are caused.

72. Sections 9th and 10th are considerations of God's prescience. The argument, which is elaborated at great length, seems in substance to be this: God foreknows all the future phenomena of the universe; this foreknowledge renders or proves them certain and necessary. No intellect can foreknow except by means of the chain of causes which precede the event. Even if they were not immediately preceded by causes, they are so necessarily connected with God's prescience as to be inconsistent with the scheme of liberty, which is to be without all necessity.

73. There are several errors in this argument which render it worthless. The first error we will notice is that no intellect can foresee future events except by means of the antecedent causes. True, *man* cannot; but it is a strange proceeding to measure *God's* mind by *man's*. This foreknowledge proves them certain and necessary (in the absolute sense of the term). And further; even if there is no being to foreknow future events, still every phenomena that ever will take place in the future progress of time will take place in a *certain* time and manner, and any being could foresee it who *had the requisite sagacity* or faculty; and this would be true even if the universe were jumbled

to chaos, and even the law of causation annihilated. I shall not prove this proposition, for it is self-evident. On close inspection it will be found to be but a mere truism; the whole is contained in the hypothetical part that certain events " will take place in the future;" for if they will take place they will take place in a certain manner, and prescience can foresee them. But all this does not touch the issue of liberty and necessity. That issue is, have volitions immediate antecedent causes? Prescience is perfectly consistent with the affirmative or negative of this question.

PART II.

74. Section 1st is a consideration of the idea that moral character can attach to no action which is not free. He argues that the virtuousness or viciousness consists, not in the *cause*, but in the *nature* of the act. He says, "the thing which makes sin hateful is that by which it deserves punishment, which is but the expression of hatred;" and "that which renders virtue lovely is the same with that, on account of which it is fit to receive praise and reward, which are but the expression of esteem and love." I will but simply remark that I do not think punishment an expression of hatred, but a means of exciting in the mind of the delinquent a motive to do right, and thereby using the only means of remedying his deficient moral state. While milder means will effect the end, punishment proper, or such as is painful to the person punished, should not be resorted to. "Expressing hatred" as such, does no good either to the community or individual, and if moral acts are necessitated by a long chain of causes extending far back of the person, it is hard to say he deserves such punishment as is painful to him, aside from the necessary protection of society and his own reformation. I suppose punishment is mainly for the good of the person punished. He has defective moral faculties. The process of enlargement is painful, but like a man with a hare-lip, this process of amendment is for his good. I must close with these naked statements; it is not the place for a treatise on ethics.

APPENDIX.

CHAPTER I.

AN INQUIRY INTO THE NATURE OF THE MORAL FACULTIES.

1. A knowledge of the nature, authority, and legitimate action of the moral faculties must be of the first importance to an organized society. These faculties, more than any other, fit man for the social state. Fully impressed with the responsibility of the task, it is undertaken with trembling solicitude. In addition to the intrinsic difficulty of the subject, it is so metaphysical in its nature, and has occupied so little of the *attention* of mankind, that with all possible painstaking, an author is liable to be *not* understood, and to be *mis*-understood. And more especially is this the case where there is a studied brevity that condenses pages to a sentence. Should the developments of time show that some grains of error have been intermingled with the following ideas, the author has two sources of consolation; first, that his intentions were honest; second, that no previous writer on the subject can "cast the first stone." All attempts to develop and elucidate a satisfactory system of morals will prove abortive, if not based on fundamental notions of the nature and destiny of man, and the *objects* of his creation. The following system has two foundations, one of which is acknowledged to be hypothetical; the other is claimed to be made of the facts of observation. We now present the first

PLATFORM OR PREMISE OF A MORAL SYSTEM.

2. This consists of notions which most monotheists, and all Christians, have always embodied among their fundamental notions of theology. For this and other reasons, no attempt will be made to establish the premise, but only

to show that the conclusions are legitimately and irresistibly deduced from the premise. The premise is simply that Deity is, and has been, since a period long anterior to the creation of aught besides, infinitely benevolent. That benevolence is one of his predominant characteristics. The only ultimate object of the action of a benevolent agent must be happiness. This may be called pleasure, enjoyment, satisfaction, well-being, etc.; but the *idea* (with which we have to deal) remains the same. This proposition appears so self-evident as to render any argumentation, by way of proof, very difficult. The only *ultimate* good is happiness; all other good is relative, and it is only valuable as it conduces to this end. Of what possible use, benefit, or good are fine houses, statues and paintings, sunny skies and fertile fields, if there are no sentient beings to enjoy them? Of what advantage are a fine physical frame and symmetrical limbs if there be no conscious spirit to control and enjoy them? Of what benefit is delightful music if there be no ear to enjoy it? All other good things are links in a chain, of which happiness is the terminus. Happiness is a good in itself; it is only when it causes (as it sometimes does) greater unhappiness, that it becomes an evil; and even then the happiness is equally a good, only the evil which it causes overbalances the good, and renders it worthy of avoidance. No claim is here made to originality; theologians and metaphysicians of reputation have maintained the same ideas.

3. The idea above enunciated, though not the direct object of the author, is distinctly avowed in the following quotation from Trumbull's Principles of Moral Philosophy; taken from a note to President Edwards' work on the will. "*Whence then comes evil?* is the question that hath in all ages been reckoned the *Gordian* knot in philosophy. And, indeed, if we own the existence of evil in the world in an *absolute* sense, we diametrically contradict what hath been just now proved of God. For if there be any *evil* in the system, that is not good in respect to the *whole*, then is the *whole* not good, but evil; or at best, very imperfect. And an *author* must be as his *workmanship* is; as is the effect, such is the cause. But the solution of this difficulty is at hand: That there is no evil in the universe. What! are there no pains, no imperfections? Is there no imperfection? Is there no misery, no vice in the world? Or, are not

these *evils*? Evils, indeed they are; that is, those of one sort are hurtful, and those of the other sort equally hurtful and abominable; but they are *not* evil or mischievous with respect to the *whole*. But He is at the same time said to creat evil, darkness, confusion; and yet to do no evil, but to be the author of man, but giveth to all men liberally, and upbraideth not. And by the prophet Isaiah, He is introduced, saying of Himself, I form light, and create darkness; I make peace, and create evil: I. the Lord, do all these things. What is the meaning, the plain language of all this? but I, the Lord, delighteth in goodness, and (as the scripture speaks) evil is his strange work? He intends and pursues the universal *good* of his creation, and the evil which happens is not permitted for its own sake, or through any pleasure in evil, but because it is requisite to the greater good pursued."

4. President Edwards, in his essay on the will, advances a similar idea on the following quotation: "There is no inconsistency in supposing that God may hate a thing as it is in itself, and considered simply as evil, and yet that it may be his will it should come to pass, considering all consequences. I believe, there is no person of good understanding, who will venture to say, he is certain that it is impossible it should be best, taking in the whole compass and extent of existence, and all consequences in the endless series of events, that there should be such a thing as moral evil in the world. And if so, it will certainly follow, that an infinitely wise being, who always chooses what is best, must choose that there should be such a thing. And if so, then such a choice is not an evil, but a wise and holy choice; and if so, then that providence which is agreeable to such a choice, is a wise and holy providence. God does not will sin as sin, or for the sake of anything evil; though it be his pleasure so to order things, that, He permitting, sin will come to pass; for the sake of the great good that by his disposal shall be the consequence. His willing to order things so that evil shall come to pass, for the sake of the contrary good, is no argument that He does not hate evil, as evil; and if so, then it is no reason why He may not reasonably forbid evil, as evil, and punish it as such." (Page 371.)

5. Professor Finney says in his Systematic Theology, the reason of moral obligation "is then the intrinsic and

infinite value of the highest good of God and of the universe, that constitutes the true foundation of moral obligation. The highest well being of God, and of the universe of sentient creatures, is the end on which preference, choice, intention, ought to terminate." "The *law* or the *lawgiver* aims to promote the higest good or blessedness of the universe. This must be the end of moral law and moral government."

6. The idea which we wish to enunciate and elucidate is clearly contained in each of the above quotations, though mingled with other ideas with which at present we have nothing to do. We wish to begin with ultimates; and we wish to show that, with God's benevolent character as a premise, happiness of the Creator and the created *must* have been the *obje t* of creation. The particulars of the moral faculties and of the moral obligation of their action we reserve for subsequent investigation, based, not on hypotheses of the character of the Creator, but an observation of their nature. It is contrary to reason that a benevolent Creator should enjoy as much happiness from the misery of his creatures as their happiness. From the above premise we are prepared to enunciate the following conclusion: that *the nature of the moral faculties, and their strength pro-proportionate to the other faculties, are such, considering the imperfect state and development of man, as best to promote the highest happiness of God's creatures*. If the wisdom of Deity could, previous to creation, have discovered any other *quality* or *degree* of moral faculty that, if inserted into man as he is, and as he is situated, would have resulted in more happiness, what *reason* could he have had for not doing it?

7. Bishop Butler in his "Analogy" maintains the opposite theory—that we can have no idea of the object of God in creation. He says, in substance (I am obliged to quote from memory, not having access to his work), that man can have no conception of the object or end of creation. This is clearly announced and illustrated by a strong comparison. It is readily admitted that if we know not what his predominant attributes or qualities are, or if He have attributes or qualities of which we have no conception, we can know nothing of his objects. But theologians assume to know these; and if so, logic compels certain conclusions.

8. A few more conclusions remain to be deduced from the above premise. And it may be well here to announce

that we shall undertake to prove that there are two kinds of morality—absolute morality or right, and relative morality or right. These are diverse from and often directly opposite each other. It appears a conclusion from the above premise that absolute morality or right consists in that conduct of each individual which, in his relation to all other beings, would result in the highest happiness. Some might add, without doing wrong to any; but this is thought unnecessary; for it is not to be admitted that an all-wise Deity has so contrived the mechanism of his creation that ultimate good can be done by wrong to any. Another inference is that a perfect intellect, able to apprehend the fact and the nature of his relations to all other beings, would see by the light of intellect the *proper* course for him to pursue without the aid of a moral faculty. Another inference is that a perfect moral faculty, legitimately cultivated and exercised, would instinctively indicate a course of conduct identical with the above, that is, calculated to promote the highest possible happiness without any aid from intellect, except such as is necessary for its action. The imperfection of the intellect raises the necessity of a moral faculty, and the imperfection of both raises the necessity of the above distinction between absolute right and relative right. When these shall coalesce, man will have attained his perfect development. When this will be, or whether ever, the writer saith not. We now come to consider, from observation of the moral faculties, the second platform.

CHAPTER II.

SECOND PLATFORM OR PREMISE OF A MORAL SYSTEM.

9. It should be borne in mind that we take as a starting point the principle that happiness, pleasure, or that which is agreeable, positively, and pain or unhappiness, negatively, are the only actual or possible motives to human action, and the only ultimate ends of human existence or effort; and other things are good only as they cause, directly or indirectly, present or remote happiness. It seems to be self-evident, and for that reason to forbid proof by any pro-

cess of ratiocination; for reason as long as we will, our reasoning must commence with premises or first principles which are assumed as starting points. Every thought and emotion of the mind must be either agreeable, disagreeable, or neutral. If agreeable it invites volition, if disagreeable it repels it, and if neutral it can scarcely exert an influence. Milton's demon may have truly said, "Evil, be thou my good," but his constitution was such that he took pleasure in that which, by the government under which he lived, caused greater pain; and he had not sufficient foresight, moral principle, and self-control to avoid the greater evil.

HAPPINESS, WHAT?

10. Happiness is an agreeable state of mind consequent on an action of some power of the mind. Strictly speaking, there is no such thing as "bodily pain." The pain is in the mind, and is caused by a disordered state of the body. The healthy or normal action of any faculty occasions the highest happiness of which it is capable without excessive action, which either impairs its power of contributing happiness or causes a painful action of other faculties. The greatest good of mankind is the highest happiness of which the race is capable. Good men are ready to admit that the constitution and relation of our nature are such that each one contributes most to the general good by that course which is best calculated to secure his own happiness.

THE HIGHEST PERSONAL HAPPINESS.

11. *Is caused by the most perfect symmetrical development and exercise of all the powers of our being.* This proposition will hardly encounter opposition, for it is little more than a truism. It is not said what *is* a symmetrical development of each faculty; it is not said how much time and strength should be devoted to the cultivation or exercise of any faculty to give it a due proportionate development. It will not readily be believed that there are any faculties which are superfluous or which do not contribute to the general good of the person; that the legitimate action of any faculty is painful, or that the appropriate action of any faculty infringes on the happy action of any other faculty. The circumstances of an individual often forbid symmetrical development, his occupation requiring the dispropor-

tionate development of some particular faculty; but this is not against the general idea above stated.

ULTIMATE MORALITY.

12. The same distinction between absolute morality and relative morality, which was inferred from the character of Deity, is thought to be a logical conclusion from the facts above stated. *Ultimate or absolute morality is that conduct for each person which in the circumstances in which he is placed, all things and all times being considered, will do most to promote the happiness of mankind and their Creator.* Relative morality is that conduct which, in the relations he sustains to others, is, as to him, right in the eyes of an omniscient being, and will excuse him from blame. Ultimate morality can be known only by a perfect intellect and a perfect moral faculty, and therefore *is* known only to the omniscient Deity; yet it is the point which all should strive for; that is, they should strive so to cultivate all their faculties as to come as near to it as possible. The second rule leads different persons to different conduct, and even to that which is directly opposite, explaining facts that everywhere exist. Before answering the pertinent query, How can we ascertain the second rule in practical life? it will be necessary to give an exposition of the nature of the

MORAL FACULTY.

13. *The moral faculty is that power of the mind which, in all conduct which may affect the happiness of others, awakens the sentiment of moral obligation.* The sentiment of right, or moral obligation, exists, with greater or less distinctness, in all men who have not stupefied it by crime. To say that this is produced by a certain power of mind, is nothing more than to say, that the mind has power to exercise or produce such a sentiment. It is not saying whether the mind produces this sentiment by acting as a whole, or by the action of a particular part of the substance or essence of the immaterial mind, or the brain through which it acts. This question presents no issue which has anything to do with the practical nature of the sentiment, and therefore is not entitled to discussion at present.

14. A little reflection will suffice to convince any one,

that the moral faculty is the parent of the sentiment; and the moral sentiment of the words should, ought, etc., expressing the sentiment. The sentiment or idea must have existed previous to the word expressing it; the sentiment of sublimity was the originator of the word. The words "color," "red," "blue," and "olive" would be impossible and useless in their present sense, had not the perceptions of colors existed previous to the word, and had not the mind power to produce them again. The words music, harmony, and melody would be useless had the mind no musical faculty; the same is true of any word expressing the action of any simple uncombined faculty. The intellect can judge of the expediency—policy of an action; or its tendency to produce happiness; but this is different from oughtness which can only be given by the moral faculty. A certain amount of intellectual action is necessary to enable one of these simple faculties to act. The faculty of sublimity cannot act unless the intellect takes up the outlines of a sublime object. All metaphysicians agree, that the instinctive or natural action of each simple faculty of the mind produces in all men the same mental state, or sentiment, differing only in the degrees of intensity. If this be true, the moral faculty enforces in all men, the same circumstances, the same conduct. But this is notoriously contrary to fact. One man eats meat on Friday conscientiously, and another with as good a conscience abstains. Nothing is more common than for men's conscience to conflict. Yet it is a simple faculty. How is this apparent contradiction to be explained?

15. The explanation is ready, and we think will be satisfactory. As before stated, a certain amount of intellectual action is necessary, as a condition of the action of all the simple faculties of the mind. The outlines of an object must be perceived before it can be pronounced, by the action of the faculty of sublimity, to be sublime or otherwise. The amount of intellectual action necessary to the action of some faculties is greater than for others. A small amount of intellectual action is sufficient for the action of the faculties of color, and music; more for the action of sublimity, and beauty; and still more for the action of the moral faculties. Previous to the action of the moral faculties, there must be an action of all those powers of mind that impart a knowledge of, and constitute the relations of the person to all others whom his conduct may affect. This relation to

others, consists not simply in the external circumstances of the person, but in the state of each other faculty, *conspicuous among which are men's religious and moral beliefs*. These are not alike in any two persons, and in many they are the reverse; hence the moral sentiment must necessarily be different in different persons. We may now consider the means of the

CULTIVATION OF THE MORAL FACULTY.

16. The moral faculty, being a simple faculty of the mind, acting instinctively, or spontaneously, that is, by the force of its own nature, when the conditions are supplied, the laws of its cultivation are similar to those of other faculties. It should be kept in mind, that the natural action of all the primary or simple faculties are the same in all men and in all ages. This is an admitted principle, and must be so, else all scientific knowledge of mind is at an end. All, then, that the cultivation of the moral faculty, simply as such, can do, is, not to change or reverse the approvals or disapprovals, but to increase the distinctness, power, and delicacy of its emotions. The most stupid clown does not think harmony discord, or melody harshness; nor does he think a sublime or a beautiful object the reverse. But those who have cultivated these faculties, have a much stronger and more delicate action of them. Every one knows that the way to cultivate any power of mind, is, to exercise it with system and perseverance. He who wishes to cultivate the logical faculty, plies himself to solving the problems and demonstrating the theorems of Euclid. He who would improve his musical powers composes music, sings, and plays instruments of music. The obvious way, then, to cultivate the moral faculty, is, *carefully to consult the moral sense in every act involving moral principle*. If the object of action be, as it too often is, to gain the applause and approbation of our fellow-men, or to gain wealth, irrespective of the action of the moral sense, it is not cultivated, but rather stupefied. We now come to consider an important part of our subject, namely, how we may ascertain, for practical life, as to one's self,

THE RULE OF RIGHT.

17. As the moral faculties, as shown above, act on the

materials furnished by the intellect, consisting of the relations apprehended or supposed to be apprehended, the moral sense will be according to the state of the intellect. The method of ascertaining the rule of right in any given case is to enlighten the intellect as far as may be as to the relations one sustains to other beings. One should avail himself of all means within his reach—the Bible, the conversations of wise men who have considered these things, books of casuistry, and all other means of informing the intellect. But one must depend on his own judgment as to the books he shall consult, the importance he shall attach to their teachings, and, in the last resort, his conscience will act upon the material so furnished to it by his intellect. If it be asked how we are to know that this diligence ought to be used, I answer that common sense and conscience teach that proper exertion ought to be made to ascertain duty. When the conscience thus acts, its decisions are peremptory and final, without appeal and without exception. It is the rule of right to which his conduct should conform; and by which he ought to be judged by all moral tribunals. If he does not conform to the rule of absolute right (as is often the case), it is owing to the imperfection of his faculties. He has done his best to ascertain that rule. If this is not his rule of right, he has no means of ascertaining it, and must *guess* in the dark. If one has impaired his faculties, he may have sinned in so doing, but it would be contrary to the common sense and cultivated reason of mankind, to demand what is beyond his present capacity to accomplish. If the above rule is not correct, it is impossible to ascertain duty. If a person believes in any supernatural or natural code of morals, his conscience would enforce it. Some have contended that men sometimes do wrong when acting according to the distinct dictation of conscience; but this is owing to a confusion of ideas consequent on not making the above distinction between absolute morality and relative morality. It is seen that men's consciences are different and reverse from each other; it is believed right is identical and unchangeable. In reconciling these ideas they are led into error. If it is ever right to act counter to conscience, the cases should be carefully pointed out; but what writer on casuistry ever undertook such a task? Let him who thinks it right to violate conscience, undertake to point out the precise circumstances in which it should be done. Besides, if conscience is not a rule of moral conduct, we have no means of ascertaining duty; for the decisions of our best judgment are a basis on which conscience acts.

The voice of poets (who are thought to be more truthful expositors of human nature than theorists) is not wanting to substantiate the foregoing ideas. One says:

"He that does the best his circumstances allow,
Does well, acts nobly, angels could do no more."

Another not unknown to fame says:

"Whatever creed be taught or land be trod,
The voice of conscience is the voice of God."

Another of a still greater fame as a Christian writer says:

"What conscience dictates to be done,
Or warns me not to do;
This teach me more than hell to shun,
That more than heaven pursue."

18. We have thus given the fundamental principles of a system of morals. To apply these to practical life would be foreign to our purpose, and would swell this volume beyond its prescribed limits. Besides, every moral act rests on its own merits, and were all these given, the "world itself could not contain the books that should be written." It is more feasible and practical to prove first principles, so that each one can, by their help, ascertain his duty in every conceivable circumstance. We here fully adopt the following doctrine and language of President Mahan in the preface to his Moral Philosophy. He says: "The *uncertainty* which commonly attends disquisitions in Moral Philosophy is owing, as it appears to me, to the reason stated above—the want of well-settled ideas of the true end and aim of such a science. Let it once be understood that its sphere is not to specify, in a formal manner, the varied duties of man; not to decide whether such and such particular courses of conduct are wright or wrong, but to furnish and elucidate universal formulas or principles, in the light of which all such questions may be answered by the student for himself, and then moral philosophy will take its place, not among the uncertain, but the certain sciences."

It is earnestly hoped that the brevity with which these

principles have been enunciated and elucidated will not lead to their misapprehension; if any carelessly or willfully misconstrue them, their sin be upon their own head. Owing to its intrinsic importance, in the light of the foregoing principles, we subjoin the following consideration of human or national governments.

CHAPTER III.

HUMAN OR NATIONAL GOVERNMENTS.

19. Governments are necessary to secure and promote the highest happiness of the governed; therefore they are right. Good governments are desirable, but poor ones better than none; even tyranny is better than anarchy. Therefore, governments should be obeyed, with the following exceptions:

(1.) As governments are instituted and sustained to protect life, liberty, property, and such pursuits of happiness as do not infringe on the rights of others; whenever they become destructive of these ends, it is the right of the people to alter or abolish them! Revolution, rebellion, and secession are rights inherent in the people. What extent of grievance will justify, or what prospect of forming a better government will warrant them, is matter for sound discretion. That such is the belief of Americans since the Revolution, is well attested each Fourth of July.

(2.) When the mandates of government are contrary to the dictates of conscience. If the foregoing principles are true, there is no exception to the principle that the dictate of conscience is the rule of duty or conduct for the individual.

In such a case, when conscience is obeyed and law violated, one of three courses must be taken. The person must quietly submit to the penalty of the law, or escape it by stealth, or openly resist it. As either is right, it is a matter of discretion which shall be taken. The first proves the sufferer's sincerity, and exerts a powerful moral influence. The second is justifiable on the score of self-preservation. The third, in case the intention is to reform government, amounts to rebellion; and the above remarks will apply; if the intention is to sacrifice the resisters as martyrs, it is matter of discretion whether such is the best course.

20. The following remarks on this subject, found in Macaulay's "History of England" (pp. 305), are worthy of consideration. This justly approved writer, making no pretension to casuistry, speaks as a practical man and a historian He says: "It is true that to trace the exact boundary between rightful and wrongful resistance is impossible; but this impossibility arises from the nature of right and wrong, and is found in almost every part of ethical science. A good action is not distinguished from a bad action by marks so plain as those which distinguish a hexagon from a square. There is a frontier where virtue and vice fade into each other. Who has ever been able to define the exact boundary between courage and rashness, between prudence and cowardice, between frugality and avarice, between liberality and prodigality? Who has been able to say how far mercy to offenders ought to be carried, and where it ceases to deserve the name of mercy and becomes a pernicious weakness? What casuist, what lawgiver, has ever been able to mark nicely the limits of the right of self-defense? All our jurists hold that a certain quantity of risk to life or limb justifies a man in shooting or stabbing an assailant: but they have long given up in despair the attempt to describe in precise words, that quantity of risk. They only say it must be, not a slight risk, but a risk such as would cause serious apprehension to a man of firm mind; and who will undertake to say what is the precise amount of apprehension which deserves to be called serious, or what is the precise texture of mind which deserves to be called firm? It is doubtless to be regretted that words and the nature of things do not admit of more accurate legislation; nor can it be denied that wrong will often be done when men are judges in their own cause, and proceed instantly to execute their own judgment. Yet who would, on that account, interdict all self-defense? The right which a people has to resist a bad government bears a close analogy to the right which an individual, in the absence of legal protection, has to slay an assailant. In both cases the evil must be grave. In both cases all regular and

peaceable modes of defence must be exhausted before the aggrieved party resorts to extremities. In both cases an awful responsibility is incurred. In both the burden of proof lies on him who has ventured on so desperate an expedient; and, if he fails to vindicate himself, he is justly liable to the severest penalties. But in neither case can we absolutely deny the existence of the right. A man beset by assassins is not bound to let himself be tortured and butchered, without using his weapons, because nobody has been able precisely to define the amount of danger which justifies homicide. Nor is society bound to endure passively all that tyranny can inflict, because nobody has been able precisely to define the amount of misgovernment which justifies rebellion." As an important adjunct of morals and government, we subjoin the following considerations of

PUNISHMENT OR RETRIBUTION.

21. Of that punishment which Deity may inflict after death, for moral delinquencies before, we have nothing to say. This is a question of theology, and to theologians we shall leave it. This punishment emanates from the Divine Will, and nothing respecting it can be known with definite certainty, except by revelation, or some positive communication from Deity; except what can be inferred from his character. If we know his *character*, the *end* or *object* of his actions is matter of logical inference; and if our intellect is sufficient to judge of the applicability of means to that end, we can determine, at least negatively, that He will not use means nowise adapted to accomplish the end. The fact that at death our being undergoes a great modification, and that we have no means of knowing precisely what our faculties will be after that change, seems to ignore all precise argumentation from this to that. Perhaps it is partly owing to this that the sincere believers in revelation construe it to teach so many different ideas with regard to future punishment. The most that philosophy can say is, that so long as existence remains, so much of our present constitution will remain as is necessary to preserve identity: and this is enough to show conclusively that a virtuous life will much more conduce to a capacity for happiness after death than a vicious one.

22. That punishment which national governments inflict

for the violation of its laws, should, as far as practicable, correspond with right or morality. The object is the same —human happiness. The object of punishment, then, is protection of society and reformation of the criminal. Those means should be used which are best adapted to these ends. The details of such treatment are foreign to the objects of this work.

23. Aside from the outward and tangible punishment of vice, the keen and delicate relish of virtuous action is gradually destroyed. And the more any faculties are unduly developed and exercised, which alone constitutes vice, the more the person is likely to engage in that conduct which will terminate disastrously. These considerations, the most weighty if rightly viewed, and the greatest bulwark of virtue, lose their force as the mind increases in moral turpitude; hence the necessity of prisons and positive inflictions. Punishment being protective and reformatory, all excess, either in duration or degree, which does not conduce to this end, being wanton cruelty, can have no *moral* force. It may awaken the slavish fear which the vanquished has for an inexorable tyrant, but can never awaken love, respect, or confidence.

24. President Mahan, in his Moral Philosophy, says the idea of retribution " has its basis in the idea of merit and demerit, as *intrinsically* attaching to right or wrong moral action. The ill-desert attaching to wrong-doing pertains exclusively to what is intrinsic in the action itself, and does not depend at all upon the conduct of the subject *after its perpetration*. The act in itself remains what it is, and consequently its ill-desert, whatever the subsequent conduct of the perpetrator may be."

25. It is a little difficult to determine precisely what is meant by the phrase, " demerit intrinsically attaching to wright or wrong moral action." If it be meant that the *action* is the measure of moral turpitude and punishment, independent of the constitution or external circumstances of the subject acting, few will be induced to receive it. The foregoing theory is, that the reformation or future well-being of the moral delinquent, and the protection of society, is the basis of, and is identical with, "the merit or demerit *intrinsically* attaching to right or wrong moral action." The *object*, then, of retribution or punishment is, to secure good or happiness. To secure this, its necessity

has its basis in the nature of man, including his moral sense or conscience, and the constitution of that society the happiness of which his conduct may affect.

26. All facts show that some men are created or born with a constitution much more favorable to virtue or vice than others. Those who deny this are beyond the reach of argument. It is equally apparent that some are, in their helpless years, while habits and character are most rapidly formed, surrounded by circumstances more favorable to virtue, than others. To say that in a government so perfect that all these things can be known and taken into the account, as is the case with moral government, desert of punishment "attaches to what is intrinsic in the act itself," will appear to many as a flagrant violation of the very gist and end of punishment "which both from the first and now, was, and is, to" promote the highest happiness of sentient existence, and of each individual as a constituent element thereof.

27. If it be said, " severity of punishment is necessary to inspire the governed with reverence for the dignity of the government," I answer, will excessive, useless cruelty awaken in the minds of reasonable beings love and reverence for the inflictor? Or is it best to conform governments to the ideas of unreasonable men, and demons? In the above quotation the idea is clearly announced that repentance or reformation forms no ground of the omission of punishment. On the foregoing theory, a genuine reformation which is known, destroys every ground or reason of punishment.

(1.) The highest good of the offender is already effected by his reformation. The force of the example on the vicious is simply that they can escape punishment by reforming; an example that all good men would like to see followed. True, this will not exhibit the *mercy* of the Ruler; for the sternest justice can go no further. The persistence in the infliction of positive moral punishment on beings of imperfect organization, and but little experience in existence, after a sincere repentance and reformation, would be a wanton, motiveless act of tyrannical cruelty unparalleled in the acts of the Inquisition, or pandemonium; for these were prompted by selfish *ends*.

28. Human governments cannot recognize this principle, simply because they cannot distinguish between a genuine

and a feigned repentance; no such reason exists in moral government. And what harm has ever occurred, when executive clemency has released from punishment one who has given long and indubitable proof of reformation?

CHAPTER IV.

CAPITAL PUNISHMENT.

29. Contrary to my original intention, to gratify the wishes of some, I have consented to apply the foregoing abstract rules of morals and government, to this much-mooted subject. All that can be attempted is, to present a mere skeleton of the subject, leaving the reader to fill up those details which would swell this volume beyond its prescribed limits.

30. It is argued, affirmatively.

(1.) That it is the express command of God in the text, "Whoso sheddeth man's blood, by man shall his blood be shed." This text, as distinguished from Jewish national laws, is a command given to Noah, as the representative and progenitor of all posterity, and becomes binding on the race.

(2.) That it more effectually prevents murder, by the force of exemplary punishment.

(3.) That it more effectually prevents murder by depriving the murderer of the power of committing further crime.

31. Negatively, it is argued in reply to the first argument above, that no law given to Jews is binding, for if one is, all are, "which proves too much, and therefore proves nothing." (2.) That it is doubtful whether the above text is a *command*, or a mere maxim or proverb, or a prophecy. (3.) Whether it be binding on other nations. (4.) Whether it was not repealed by the Christian dispensation, even if it were a command. The second argument, so far as it is *a priori*, or from principle, is merely begging the question. History and reason concur to prove that *that* punishment which is most properly adapted or pro-

portioned to the crime, has the greatest exemplary force. An unjust degree of punishment but hardens the heart. Whether capital punishment be *adapted* to the crime is the very question at issue. Probably there has not been a sufficiently extended trial of both methods of punishment to make out a conclusive argument. So far as trial has been had, it seems, in the opinion of many, to be against capital punishment.

With our present, or more perfect state-prison arrangements, there can be but little force to the third argument.

It should be borne in mind, that if the foregoing essay develops correct principles, the proper objects of all punishment are protection of society and reformation of the criminal; therefore, all pain inflicted which is not necessary to the one, or does not tend to the other, is vindicative and wrong.

32. (1.) The first argument against capital punishment is, that the innocent sometimes suffer. Notwithstanding that, in favor of life, the law strongly favors the accused; yet it is too frequent for the innocent to be accused, tried, convicted, sentenced, executed, and afterwards proved to be so. In case of capital punishment, no restitution can be made; but in case of imprisonment by executive pardon, the unfortunate sufferer can be restored to character and liberty; and might, by legislative provision, have the pittance he has earned. This argument must have considerable weight, and can only be set aside by necessity.

(2.) The criminal has time and space for repentance and reformation. The arrangements of penitentiaries are designed, and in a good degree calculated, to quiet and repress the action of those faculties which prompt to crime and to promote the action of those which prompt to virtuous action. In most cases reformation is possible, in some actual, and in a few hopeless. On the hypothesis that probation absolutely ceases with life, and endless, unmitigable torment awaits the culprit, this consideration swells to an importance inconceivable to a finite mind.

33. (3.) The criminal, if imprisoned, may earn something for his family, if he has one (and the legislature may give it them); if not, he may earn something for the State.

(4.) In case of imprisonment punishment can be made a little more certain than in case of hanging; such is the feeling of juries and executive functionaries; and as Blackstone truly says, in substance, the exemplary force of punishment depends not so much on its *severity* as on its *certainty*. Murderers, almost exclusively, either expect to escape punishment or are driven by their passions to such desperation that they are willing to sacrifice themselves. In England, when a great number of petty crimes were punished with death, those crimes were astonishingly prevalent. If, in the nature of mind, and in the nature of things external to the mind, imprisonment be more proportioned to the crime than death, then its exemplary force as a preventive of murder will be greater. On principle, *a priori*, this is thought to be the case; a sufficiently extended trial has probably not taken place to prove it, *a posteriori*, from facts.

CHAPTER V.

OF PERSONAL IDENTITY.

34. Personal identity may be considered under two divisions: First, the fact or existence of identity; second, the knowledge, evidence, or proof of identity. *Personal identity* may be said to consist of *a constitution of our nature by which there is some degree of similarity and causative influence between the successive mental states or thoughts, feelings, and volitions.*

(1.) There is not a precise similarity in body or mind at any two different periods of time. There is a great dissimilarity between the young babe and the veteran ready to sink into the grave, yet they are the same identical person. Identity must be either of the constitution or of the constituent substance. It cannot be an identity of the constituent elements of the physical system; for physiologists agree that these are constantly changing, and that there is an entire change once in seven years. It cannot be identity of the constituent elements of mind, for if mind is an attenuated form of matter, the elementary particles of matter will change with those of the physical system; but if mind be spiritual and immaterial, it is beyond the cognizance of our faculties, except by consciousness, which can give us no information on the subject. Since, then, it cannot be identity of constituent substance, and since there is not a complete sameness at successive periods, identity must be such a constitution as produces some degree of similarity between the successive mental states. This can only be uniformly produced by some causative influence in the antecedents over the subsequents.

35. It is conceived that philosophy can afford no solution of the question whether mind is material or immaterial in its organization. Most physiologists admit that mind in its manifestations is dependent on, and affected by, the organized matter of the brain and nervous system, *as if it were part and parcel of that vitalized matter.* It is said by the materialist that "death destroys this organization, and consequently all power of mental manifestation." But what proof have they that there is not an immaterial substratum capable of mental manifestation dependent on the organization of the physical system during its connection therewith, but self-acting afterwards? Or what evidence have they that, if mind be material, on the dissolution of the more gross and tangible part of our physical systems a more refined and attenuated form of material organization may not remain capable of manifesting mind?

36. (2.) The knowledge or proof of identity is made out by the testimony of consciousness and memory. At each successive period we are conscious of certain mental states; by consciousness we know that our present memory is a part of ourselves. This memory links together the successive conscious states, convincing that they all belonged to us. No one doubts the truthfulness of memory when legitimately exercised. It being a single power or faculty of the mind, like all other simple mental faculties, its legitimate conclusions must be taken as final or all knowledge and reasoning must come to an end. But it is said "that memory is often erroneous." I answer, so are the most simple faculties of observation. Persons often differ in regard to the color and shape of objects they have both seen; but this is owing, not to the fallibility of the faculties themselves, but their hurried, confused, and imperfect exercise, by which a wrong idea is had at the time. So it is with memory; if it ever err, it is owing to an imperfect exercise at the time the impression is made, or a subsequent diseased or decayed state of the physical system sufficient to produce some degree of mental unsoundness.

37. Although identity includes all that comes within the sphere or pale of consciousness, yet all of consciousness is not essential to identity or the person. We may ascertain the extent of identity by seeing what part may be removed without destroying the person. Either of our limbs may be removed and identity still remain; so any part of the physical system may be removed without destroying identity which does not destroy the vitality of such system. It will readily be conceded that the physical system cannot live without the mental, and that it is not absurd for the mental to exist after the physical system is dissolved; therefore identity must be in the mind, and not in the matter that surrounds it. If we examine still further we shall find that some faculties of mind may be removed without destroying identity or the person. In some persons, not deficient in intellect, some faculties are almost wanting. George Combe, although a great philosopher, was so destitute of the faculty of calculation that he never could learn the multiplication table. If we continue this trimming process we shall find that any faculty can be removed and identity still remain, until we destroy one of the three great departments of mind—the intellect or knowing part, the sensibility or department of desire and feeling or emotion, and the will or acting part. If either of these is gone, the person or identity is broken up. If intellect be wanting, desire is totally blind as to the means of its own gratification, or even of sustaining existence; if desire were wanting, whatever be the knowledge, there could be no motive to action; and if the will be wanting, though intellect and desire are full, yet no action could take place in accordance with the one or in gratification of the other. Therefore, whatever changes have taken place in the past or may in the future, we may safely say that some degree of intellect, sensibility, and will are necessary to continue personality.

38. The question has been asked, "Do persons think in a sound sleep?" It would seem that any definition of "thought" is defective that does not include consciousness. Thought may be defined to be a conscious succession or variation of mental phenomena. This may be illustrated by the phenomenon of physical pain, which is a disagreeable feeling or sensation caused by a disordered state of the physical system. Can pain exist without our being conscious of it? All the physical phenomena may exist in

the hand when the nerve connecting it with the brain is severed or paralyzed; yet as the proper "I," or person is bounded and limited by consciousness, if there be pain it is that of the hand, and not of the person; or, more properly speaking, it is but an antecedent part of what would be pain if it were not for the separation of the hand from the person; so, while consciousness is suspended, as in a swoon or sound sleep, all the phenomena of thought may occur in the brain; but these physical movements are only an antecedent part of thought until it comes to consciousness. We are entirely unable to say whether there be mental phenomena beyond the sphere of consciousness, as this is all the power we have of investigating mind; and by hypothesis this is dormant. But this we can say, that if there be mental phenomena they are but a part of the thought of the person and are detached, existing "on their own hook," as some philosophers say men are, being a spark struck off from Deity.

CONCLUSION.

39. It may be said "that the principle of the foregoing work, is too simple to apply to so profound an object as *mind*. It does not look reasonable that the multifarious mental operations, the sublime and religious emotions, the profound reasonings, and the tender and gushing affections should all conform to the simple law of causation, or of uniformity of consequent with a similar antecedent." To this it may be said, that truth is simpler than error and falsehood. A thousand false representations may be made of a single occurrence, but only one true one. False philosophy is always more complicated than that which is true; and not unfrequently has the true been rejected, in the progress of science, an account of its simplicity. Alchemy was believed in, and pursued by the learned, for long centuries, in the expectation of finding the philosopher's stone, and the means of transforming the baser metals into gold. Even Lord Bacon's vast and penetrating mind did not escape the general contagion. Yet the phantom of alchemy was much more complex than the true science of chemistry, which reduces the action and combination of chemical agents, to general laws, which are ascertained by experiment. Astrology, which pervaded antiquity, through its

most scientific periods, remnants of which are still discernible in the popular superstitions, was vastly more complicated than astronomy, its scientific successor. This explains the vast, beautiful, and complicated movements of the entire planetary system, by a simple law which every clown understands. Monotheistic Christianity is more simple than polytheistic idolatry. Much scientific research has proved fruitless on account of overlooking the simplicity of truth and nature.

40. It may be said, "the foregoing theory reduces man to a level with the brute." In answer it may be asked, Of what faculties does it deprive man? Does it not leave him all his sublime moral, religious, and beautiful emotions, and his God-like reason? Do not these, together with the greater perfection of all his faculties, sufficiently distinguish him from lower animals? It leaves him as it finds him. It deprives him of no faculty or destiny, to which he was before entitled.

41. Again it may be said that "the foregoing theory makes man a mere machine, depriving him of the power of acting only as he is caused to act." True an attempt has been made to detect a resemblance in this, that while one is a thing of *law*, the other is not a being of blind, chaotic chance. But it is thought that no great acumen is required to discern a distinction in the noble powers of thought, deliberation, choice, affection, and in some measure of self-action, as a part of motive is himself. True we think, in a certain sense, he has not the power of acting differently from his pleasure or choice, until his pleasure or choice are changed, but can this be a hardship?

42. Again it may be said that "it destroys the morality, rightness or wrongness, of conduct and character." I answer, by no means. We may differ slightly as to the precise meaning of these terms; and still more as to the treatment of those to whom they apply. But our vision is too obtuse to see why, on that account, *you* have a better right to say *we* destroy them, than *we* have to say *you* destroy them. Moral wrong or blamableness, is a term which is used to designate or describe one who is deficient in moral faculties, as evidenced by his conduct. When a man will pusillanimously fly from the least threatening of danger, we say he is a coward. When a person exhibits great attachment and tenderness towards his wife and children, we

say he is affectionate So of other qualities. And when a man is dishonest in his dealings, we estimate him as an immoral man. We regard him with a kind of disgust, because this deficiency, more than any other, renders him dangerous to society. But we ought to suppress this feeling, if by so doing we can supply the defect. Our treatment ought to be that which will best restore the deficient faculty.

43. Again it may be said, "Reason as much as you will, I shall believe I am a free agent." I answer, no one has disputed this, or wishes to dispute it. The question is not whether *you* are free, but whether your *will* is free from the other part of yourself, or the person. Writers agree that all the processes of the vital economy of the human system, both physical and mental, except that of volition, are conformed to and governed by the law of causation. But with regard to the latter important mental operation, there has ever been great diversity of opinion. Whatever the truth may ultimately appear to be, a sincere and somewhat patient effort has been made to ascertain the truth in this matter, by investigating on the principle of observation and induction. The writer was educated in the doctrine of freedomists, which was at first cherished. But ere the close of the course of lectures, he saw, or thought he saw, that they did not analyze to ultimates; or produce sound arguments to sustain their position. Years intervened before the subject appeared in the light presented in the foregoing work. And (if so much of personality may be excused) it has been prepared under very unfavorable circumstances. Metaphysical treatises have generally been written by those who have taught mental philosophy for years in a college or higher seminary. Without such an advantage, this has been written while the author was borne down by disease and debility, and struggling to become established in an arduous profession, in which he had had no previous experience. This is not said to excuse errors in doctrine. If the *principles* are false no indulgence is craved or expected; if the *mode of their presentation* is not as perfect as it might have been, a generous public will do what is generous.

44. The writer intended to present an extended examination and comparison of the writings of John Locke and Cousin, who have respectively stood at the head of English and French metaphysicians. But protracted ill-

health put it beyond his power to do so in time for this edition.

CHAPTER VI.

PHRENOLOGY AND FREE WILL.

It may not be out of place, to make a few observations respecting the relations of the foregoing doctrine of the will, to the popular and wide-spreading system of phrenology. The essential propositions of phrenology are, that the brain is the organ of the mind—that the power and kind of mental manifestation depend on its developments—that each kind of mentality, as thought, emotion, and affection, has a particular organ, in a particular part of the brain—that the relative strength of these mental faculties depends on the size and activity of their respective organs—that character and conduct depend on these latter, and that a practiced and skillful phrenologist can ascertain these with an accuracy sufficient for practical purposes, by passing the hands over the cranium. It must be obvious to every one, that the action of these several organs, and the external objects that excite them, constitute what metaphysicians term the motive or antecedent to volition. It is readily admitted that if volition is not caused, the relative strength of these several faculties may be ascertained phrenologically, without contradicting anything heretofore advanced. President Mahan, who is an unswerving defender of uncaused volition, uses the following language: "Now, it is universally admitted by philosophers of all schools, that in respect to all states and acts of the physical system, and also in respect to all mental states, intentions excepted, in respect to all states of the sensibility and intelligence, for example, man is wholly subject to the law of necessity. In respect to intentions [volitions] is he free" (from causation). But with respect to volitions, physical actions, and all those mental states, such as habitual character and conduct, which are dependent on volition, no judgment can be made, if volitions are absolutely contingent, and uncaused by these antecedent developments of thought and feeling. It is only on the hypothesis of an unvarying connection between the external developments of the cranium, and volition, that by examining the former, the latter, or anything dependent on it, can be ascertained. Now if this connection, which constitutes the causation of volition, does not exist, the sphere of phrenology must be narrowed so as to destroy its utility, if not its existence as a science.

It is sometimes objected, both to phrenology and to the doctrine of caused volition, "that frequently there is a sudden change of general volitions, of character from bad to good, and the reverse." True, but these changes are so unfrequent as to be exceptions to the general rule, that men will in the future exhibit the characteristics which they have done in the past. Such is the prevalence of this rule, that all prudent men readily trust the good man in various ways, and refuse to trust the bad one. And generally there is a full and apparent cause for this change, in the external relations and circumstances of the reformed person; and where there is no such *apparent* cause, it is by no means conclusive that one does not exist, in some unknown circumstances, or the internal working of his own mind. For example, an Irishman is in the habit of drinking to beastly inebriation, whenever he can get sufficient whisky to produce it. But suddenly he becomes temperate, and remains so, through the most trying temptations. But the auspicious change is fully accounted for by the fact, that Father Mathew, by the charming spell of his reputation, eloquence, and goodness, induced him to take the pledge of total abstinence. If any such cause exists, the objection is answered; but if a case is pointed out where no such exists, apparent or latent, the objection is valid.

SCIENTIFIC INDICATIONS OF PROGRESSION.

Delivered in Congress Hall, San Francisco, and Published in 1867.

Your attention is invited to a consideration of the universal law and fact of progression. By progression is meant the continual passing of all forms of matter and being from that which, relative to our finite minds, is cruder and lower, to the refined and higher—from the more simple to the more complex. It may be well to note some of the salient points in the unwritten history of nature's outgrowth, which indicate the past action of this universal law, unlimited by time, unbounded by space, and which therefore includes humanity as an integral portion.

There are people of sharp powers of observation, who, looking at past historic periods with that enchantment which distance lends to the view, and seeing here and there the decadence of families, tribes, and nations, feeling the wide distance between the ideal and the actual standard of moral attainment, and seeing the prevalence of want and misery, vice and venality, really believe that man is retrograding.

Humanity's progression may be compared to a mighty river, swollen by the rains or melting snows, as it rolls on its resistless current from the mountains to the sea. Here and there a rock, a headland, or a curve will form an eddy, causing the drift-wood to float swiftly in a counter-current toward the mountains. A short-sighted person, of dogmatic mind, standing on the bank, would positively declare that the course of the stream was toward the mountains;

but could his sight be extended, and the range of his vision complete, his misapprehension would be corrected.

Should any one who has thoroughly grasped the great law of progression despair, despond, or even doubt the future of humanity, either in this or spirit life, it may be accepted as a sure evidence of an aggravated dyspepsia. It it an exaggeration to say that, save our own existence, this principle is the most precious boon that the past has bequeathed to humanity? It serves to keep up a buoyant spirit, a lively hope, an abiding confidence, on which the soul can sweetly repose when the foam-capped billows of adversity are dashing around, and our immediate external environments would otherwise overwhelm us with despair.

The subject divides itself into three parts:

 I. Indications of progress from Astronomy.
 II. Indications of progress from Geology.
 III. Indications of progress from Human History.

 1. Indications from Astronomy.

We may include in this all that can be gathered in the progress of matter from its diffused, nebulous, vapory condition, until it becomes segregated and assumes the globular form, with a central sun, revolving planets, and attendant satellites.

The first question that confronts us is, are these masses of matter, which sparkle so beautifully in the depths of space, composed essentially of the same materials, and controlled by the same law of gravitation as our own planet? Fortunately the more recent attainments of astronomical science have answered both of these questions in the affirmative. By the aid of the solar spectrum and spectroscope, rays of light are analyzed and examined, and the constituent elements of the body emitting them determined. It is thus known that our sun contains iron, sodium, potassium, and other elements; and it is thus determined that the bright star Arcturus has constituent elements almost identical with our sun. And all stars indicate some of the elements common to our own globe. Thus the winged messengers—the rays of light from a twinkling star—flying across the abyss of space at the rate of 200,000 miles in a second, a rate that would leave the messages on our telegraph lines lagging at a snail's pace, after going for thousands—nay, tens of thousands of years, come to us laden with the intelligence that the globes sparkling in infinite space, are linked to the great whole by identity of constituent elements.

2d. Does the same principle of gravitation which holds each particle of matter in its place on our earth, and the earth, in its annual sweep around the sun, also obtain among the countless stars that glitter in the empyrean depths of space? We are indebted for the affirmative answer to this question to that variety in unity, which in the minor unfoldments of nature affords such pleasing gratification to the esthetic taste.

All star systems are not, like ours, composed of a central sun, and surrounding planets revolving in concentric orbits. If it were so, we should have no evidence of the continued operation of the law of gravitation beyond our system; for such is the immense distance of these sparkling orbs that even with the aid of the most powerful telescope yet in use, we are unable to discern the planets of any system. Their existence is merged in that of their parent sun, and a single orb is all that can be seen. But Sir William Herschel discovered that a considerable proportion of the fixed stars scattered through space are systems of two, of three, and sometimes more stars, revolving around a common center, thus demonstrating the universal prevalence of the law of gravitation. It is a noteworthy circumstance, that the latest discoveries of modern science should confirm— what the intuitional, mediumistic mind of Pope perceived 200 years ago, when he wrote—

"All are but parts of one stupendous whole,
Whose body nature is, and God the soul."

When Lord Rosse's large telescope swept athwart the heavens, and resolved nebulous appearances, one after another, into clusters of stars, there was great exultation among the opponents of the nebular hypothesis. They persistently claimed that those nebular masses which appeared, through the instrument, like clouds floating on the dark background of the sky, only required a more powerful telescope to be resolved likewise into star clusters. But their triumph, like that of the wicked in general, was short; for Huggins, by an application of the prism and spectroscope to the light emitted by these nebulæ, has demonstrated them to be not globes, but masses of cosmical vapor. How grand the thought that the Milky Way, whose diameter rays of light would be 1,000 years in traversing, going at the rate of twelve millions of miles in a minute, is but an aggregation of globes thrown off from a revolving mass of primordial matter, like spray from a revolving grindstone.

I will present the nebular theory in the language of one of our distinguished astronomers, to whose learning and energy we are indebted for the Cincinnati Observatory, and who lost his life nobly battling for his country in the hour of her peril. "Laplace, following up the speculations of Sir Wm. Herschel, applied the theory of that astronomer to the formation of the solar system, comprehending the comets as well as the planets and their satellites. The theory supposes the original chaotic condition of the matter of all suns and worlds was nebulous, like the matter composing the tails of comets. Under the laws of gravitation, this nebulous fluid, scattered throughout all space, commences to condense towards certain centers. The particles moving towards these central points not meeting with equal velocities, and in opposite directions, a motion of rotation is generated in the entire fluid mass, which in figure approximates the spherical form. The spherical figure once formed, and rotation commenced, it is not difficult to conceive how a system of planets might be produced from the rotating mass, corresponding in nearly all respects to the characteristics which distinguish the planets belonging to our own system. If by radiation of heat this nebulous mass should gradually contract in size, then a well-known law of rotating bodies would insure an increased velocity of rotation. This might continue until the centrifugal force, which increases rapidly with the velocity of the revolving body, would finally come to be superior to the force of gravity at the equator, and from this region a belt of nebulous fluid would thus be detached, in the form of a ring, which would be left in space by the shrinking away of the central globe. The ring thus left would generally coalesce into the globular form, and thus would present a planet with an orbit nearly, if not quite, circular, lying in a plane nearly coincident with the plane of the equator of the central body, and revolving in its orbit in the same direction in which the central globe rotates on its axis.

"As the globe gradually contracts, its velocity of rotation continually increasing, another ring of matter may be thrown off, and another planet formed, and so on, until the cohesion of the particles of the central mass may finally be able to resist any further change, and the process ceases. The planetary masses, while in the act of cooling and condensing, may produce satellites in the same manner, and by the operation of the same laws by which they were themselves formed. There are many facts which tend strongly to give this theory more than probability. It accounts for all the great features of the solar system, which in its organization presents the most indubitable evidence that it has resulted from the operation of some great law. The sun rotates on an axis in the same direction in which the planets revolve in their orbits; the planets all rotate on their axis in the same direction; they circulate around the sun, in orbits nearly circular, in the same direction, and planes nearly coincident with the plane of the sun's equator. The satellites of all the planets, with one exception, revolve in orbits nearly circular, but little inclined to the equator of their primaries, and in the same direction as the planets. So far as their rotation on an axis has been ascertained, they follow the general law. In one instance alone we find the rings of matter have solidified in cooling, without breaking up or becoming globular bodies. This is found in the rings of Saturn, which present the very characteristics which would flow from their formation, according to the preceding theory. They are flat and thin, and revolve on an axis nearly, if not exactly, coincident with that of their planet. Their stability is guaranteed by conditions of wonderful complexity and delicacy, and the adjustment of the rings to the planet (humanly speaking) would seem to be impossible after the formation of the planet. At least it is beyond our power to conceive how this could be accomplished by any law of which we have any knowledge. * * Granting the formation of a single sun by the nebular theory, and we account at once for the formation of all other suns and systems throughout all space; and according to this theory, the comets have their origin in nebulous matter, occupying positions intermediate between two or more great centers, and held nearly *in equilibrio*, until finally the attraction of some one center predominates, and this uncondensed, filmy mass commences slowly to descend toward its controlling orb. This theory would seem to be sustained—so far as a single truth can sustain any theory—by the fact that the comets come into our system from all possible directions, and pursue their courses around the sun, either in accordance with, or opposed to, the direction in which the planets circulate. Their uncondensed or nebulous condition results from the feeble central attraction which must necessarily exist in bodies composed of such small quantities of matter. Moreover, in some cases at least, there is reason to believe that in their passage around the sun they are entirely dissipated into vapor, and may thus revolve for ages, going through alternations of solidification and evaporations." Such is a brief statement of the theory that some of our first astronomers declare *more than probable*.

It is probable that the phenomena of meteoric showers, occasionally appearing about the thirteenth of November, and apparently radiating from a common center, are caused by a small incipient planet of nebulous matter impinging on our atmosphere, and portions becoming ignited by atmospheric friction, as sparks fly from steel in contact with revolving emery. Another analogous supposition is that it is caused by the minute asteroids, the fragments of an exploded planet, once between Mars and Jupiter. Through what changes or refining processes this cosmical vapor has passed, in the boundless depths of anterior eternity, is probably beyond profitable conjecture. But it appears, with all the force of a corollary, that as the acorn contains in embryonic potentiality all the qualities of the full grown oak—that is, the power to evolve in connection with favorable conditions of soil and atmosphere—so this nebulous matter contains potentially all the beautiful forms unfolded by a mature globe, with all its flora, its fauna, and the human soul its crowning ultimate.

There remains to examine one class of phenomena which have appeared as landmarks, or at least hints and indications of the vast changes that have taken place along down the stream of time. I refer to the appearance of new stars in the vacant portions of space and the permanent disappearance of old ones. More than two thousand years ago the Greek astronomer, Hipparchus, who named and numbered over one thousand stars, was astonished to find a brilliant star burst upon his view at a point in the heavens where none had existed before. But as scientific observation has been more full in modern times, cases of this kind are frequent, well marked, and established beyond a doubt.

Another class of phenomena will be best described by the following case: In 1572 a new star of great splendor appeared suddenly in the constellation Cassiopeia, occupying a position which had previously been blank. This extraordinary appearance so excited the interest of Tycho Brahe, the Danish astronomer, that he gave it his most unremitting attention. Its magnitude increased until it surpassed Jupiter in splendor and finally became visible in the daytime. It retained its greatest magnitude only a very short time, when it commenced to decline in brilliancy, changing from white to yellow, then to reddish, and finally it became faintly blue; and so diminishing by degrees it vanished from sight and has never since been seen.

While new and brilliant stars have occasionally appeared to astonish, perchance to instruct mankind, there are many well-authenticated cases of the entire disappearance of old ones whose places had been fixed with undoubted certainty. In 1690 Sir Wm. Herschel observed Star No. 55 in the constellation Hercules, but since that time no search has been able to detect it. The star is gone and its place remains a blank. Stars 80 and 81, both of the fourth magnitude in the same constellation, have likewise disappeared. Examples might be multiplied, but it is unnecessary to my purpose. I will present one other recent case, together with the light which late scientific discoveries have thrown upon it, before offering a few suggestions upon these scientific facts, which will close the first division of this essay.

In the month of May, 1866, the astronomers of various observatories in Europe and America were astonished at beholding a star in the constellation of the Northern Crown rapidly increase in size and brilliancy, passing in two weeks from the eighth to the second magnitude. Having attained its maximum, its decrease was nearly as rapid as had been its increase. It was ascertained beyond doubt by observations upon its spectrum that the star was actually wrapped in flames. Confirmatory results were obtained at the Royal Observatory of Greenwich, the Imperial Observatory of Paris, and several others.

A full account of this remarkable occurrence can be found in the October number of the *Eclectic Magazine*, in an article entitled, "A Star on Fire."

We find that nature in her ceaseless efforts towards higher forms is very prolific of new births. In the vegetable world there are vastly more blossoms than ever attain to mature fruit. As we ascend to the animal kingdom we find the efforts of nature towards reproduction are still more prolific. Should each embryonic spawn become a mature fish, the rivers, lakes, and ocean borders would become crowded to repletion. Even in the higher types of being, with all the care that affection can bestow, aided by the light of experience and science, a considerable part of humanity shuffle of the mortal coil in infancy and childhood. Is it not fair to extend this analogy to the birth of worlds?—for the infinite and the infinitesimal are subjects of the same law. May we not suppose that in the formation of a world, owing to some defect in its organization or the presence of explosive gases in its central cavity, before the crust is sufficiently hardened to insure permanence, the internal molten mass bursts forth, presenting to the astronomer the awfully grand and sublime spectacle of a star system, perhaps much larger than our own, with its planets and attendant satellites, enveloped in the flames of chemical decomposition, dissipating its substance, again to be mingled with cosmical nebulae, and thus wait for the progress of time to produce a more auspicious effort. As was beautifully expressed two hundred years ago:

> "Who sees with equal eye as God of all,
> A hero perish or a sparrow fall—
> Atoms or systems into ruin hurled,
> And now a bubble bursts, and now a world."

That which was good poetry then, is an established truth of science to-day.

Let us consider for a moment those worlds that have from time to time astonished astronomers by their appearance in the vacant fields of space.

We find in nature's unfoldments exceptional cases of growth I have this autumn seen apple trees in full bearing of excellent fruit, with here and there a blossom, and others with small apples of the second growth. So, may not the waste scraps of cosmical vapor, left from the first growth of worlds, have a rotary motion, generated by causes which we call accidental, which shall go on increasing in extent and power until a new world is born into the great family of orbs? Nay, more: As the jump of a squirrel in a snow-clad mountain will sometimes start a pellet of snow, which, as it rolls down the mountain side, increases in a geometrical ratio, until a mighty avalanche is precipitated into the valley below; so may not an angelic circle direct a shaft of magnetism upon some portion of a field of nebulous matter, thus generating a rotary motion that shall go on until a sun is launched into being, with all its planets revolving around it; which time shall people with a race of beings more moral, more healthful, more harmonious and more happy than the inhabitants of this insignificant ball shall attain to for ages to come?

Should these suggestions appear wild and extravagant, let them not detract from the value of the sterling scientific facts presented.

THE
RELIGION OF PROGRESSION.

As the matter of which the earth is composed became separated, it assumed the spherical form, and it has been mathematically demonstrated that it has the same form—being flattened at the poles and protuberant at the equator—that a molten mass would assume, when revolving at the rate that the earth is known to rotate on its axis. As has been beautifully expressed:

> "That very law which moulds a tear,
> And bids it trickle from its source,
> That law preserves the earth a sphere,
> And guides the planets in their course."

The molten mass radiated its heat until a crust of rock was formed upon its surface; radiation still went on, and as the internal mass shrunk, the external crust followed it, throwing up mountain ranges like ridges on a baked apple. These ridges were subjected to the continued wear of the elements, which may have been more active at that early period than now, and the valleys partly filled with detritus and sedimentary deposits. Thus the earth was slowly prepared for the lower types of vegetable and animal existences. The record of the gradual evolution of animal life on our planet must necessarily be exceedingly fragmentary, leaving almost every position open to objection. Two-thirds of the earth's surface is covered with water; but a small portion of the land has been examined by the geologist, and as the surface has been changed by successive elevations and depressions, and as but a small portion of animal remains were fossilized, and as much of the earlier fossils have been worn away or destroyed by the heated mass within, it is evident that a continuous record of the gradations of life can never be had. Yet geology has furnished us with sufficient facts to lead the comprehensive mind to the conclusion that life on this planet has proceeded from the lower forms or types, by a more or less regular gradation, to the higher and more complex. The leading facts, that in the oldest fossiliferous rock are found remains of invertebrates and cephelopods—animals like the cuttle-fish, with feet attached to the head—and that man is the last of the series; that of the mammalia, the marsupial, with pouch like the opossum, the lowest type appeared first; while, again, man, the highest type of the mammalia, appeared last, all point to the same conclusion. I cannot better prove and illustrate this position than to quote a passage from Hugh Miller's "Foot-Prints of the Creator," and it will have all the more weight with some minds that the author lived and died, or at least became insane, in the orthodox faith: "It is of itself an extraordinary fact, that the order adopted by Cuvier, in his Animal Kingdom, as that in which the four great classes of vertebrate animals, when marshaled according to their rank and standing, naturally range, should be also that in which they occur in the order of time. The brain, which bears an average proportion to the spinal cord of not more than two to one, comes first—it is the brain of the fish; that which bears an average to the spinal cord of two and a half to one, succeeds it—it is the brain of the reptile; then came the brain averaging as three to one—it is that of the bird; next in succession came the brain that averages as four to one—it is that of the animal; and last of all there appeared a brain that averages as twenty-three to one—reasoning, calculating man had come upon the scene." The same doctrine is advanced by Agassiz, who declares that "within the limits of the orders of each great class, there is a coincidence between their rank in organization, and the order of succession of their representatives in time."

There are three theories of the manner in which new species of life have been introduced. The Darwinian theory—that each species has been produced by the natural selection and union of the more favored individuals of the next lower species. 2. That there exist in nature monads or germ cells which, under favorable conditions, possess the inherent power of developing into a higher species. 3. That each species is produced by a special act of creation exerted by a being residing outside of nature. The advocates of the latter method often object to the theory of the development of a higher from the next lower species that there are no facts to support it; forgetting that this view would involve for living and extinct species, both animal and vegetable, four million separate acts of creation with neither reason nor a single fact to support it; only an Oriental myth to which no intelligent sectary would venture to give a literal interpretation—a myth which represents that God, standing outside of nature, labored industriously six days to create the sun, the moon, the stars, the earth, and the progenitors of animals to inhabit it; became fatigued, rested on the seventh; and that afterwards, when man, not behaving as well as he had anticipated, became derelict in his morals, repented that he had made him *and grieved himself to the heart.*

Having thus presented a synopsis of the evidence to substantiate the great fact that the external world has reached its present condition by an ascending series of growths, so we are led to the irresistible conclusion that the spiritual or religious life of the race, which is but an outgrowth or higher unfolding of the physical, is subject to the same law; that the spiritual and religious growth of Man—and by religion is meant simply a knowledge of our spirit life here and hereafter, coupled with a practical soul-culture—that the spiritual growth of man has passed with him through an ascending series of unfoldments or dispensations as he has passed from the savage to the civilized condition; that he commenced in a simple, intuitional belief in a future life, without knowledge, and at each new religion or dispensation some error is discarded and some truth added; and as the animal series has terminated and culminated man as the highest possible product of nature, so the religious has at length terminated in spiritualism, which resolves every belief into knowledge, and every special providence, every condition of spirit life, into fixed law. Spiritualism is not a sect, but a new religion; and according to the great fact and law of progression, that it is the last vouchsafed to man, is conclusive that it is the best, and that it refers everything to fixed law, shows that it must

7

terminate the series, for no unfoldment can go beyond this. There will be work enough for future ages to learn and apply to human use individual laws, but the ultimate principle is attained.

This great fact we may find illustrated by nature's processes in the growth of the individual. Nature kindly supplies childhood with a temporary set of teeth to supply the needs of that early period; but being incapable of that expansion necessary to adapt them to mature growth, she absorbs away the roots to give place to the germs beneath to furnish the permanent dentition. So every system of religion anterior to spiritualism may be considered as a provisional arrangement to meet the devotional needs of the childhood of the race, and likewise, to continue the analogy, as they are incapable of that expansion necessary to adapt them to the maturity of the race, they must all be absorbed away by nature's beautiful process, from the roots upwards, to give place to the permanent religion of spiritualism.

The physical sciences have all passed through the same phases of belief and supposition, and at length terminated in fixed law. In the dark ages supposititious alchemy was pursued with great zeal. Men spent their lives in futile efforts to find the universal solvent and methods of transmitting the baser to the more valuable metals; but these struggles resulted in the beautiful and mathematically exact science of chemistry; so supposititious and fruitless astrology culminated in the beautiful science of astronomy.

Your attention is invited to the elucidation of these views. All barbarous and savage people attribute the ordinary occurrences of life to supernatural agencies; thus, ordinary and extraordinary diseases, peace and war, floods and droughts, the abundance or scarcity of food, are all attributed to the agency of their good or bad deities. Gradually, as we descend the stream of time, and trace the slow unfoldment of man's higher intelligence, we find the supposed sphere of natural law to widen, and the sphere of the supernatural to diminish, until at length, in the full blaze of the scientific progress of the nineteenth century, the searching and comprehensive intellect of the great savant, Humboldt, anticipated the position that has been popularized by spiritualism, when he wrote in his *Cosmos:* " We become more and more convinced that the forces inherent in matter, and those which govern the moral world, exercise their action under the control of primordial necessity or fixed law." And this is the true measure of the stage of advancement of any age or any people; the extent to which they are able to trace those phenomena outworking in their own being and surroundings, to nature's immutable laws. Hence it follows, speaking in general terms, the religion of any people must bear some correspondence to their intellectual and physical attainments. And that it is practically impossible to engraft the religion of civilization upon savage or barbarous nations, any farther than they are elevated by a simultaneous introduction of the arts, the sciences, the industries, and the education of that civilization. The missionary efforts of near two centuries have resulted in little good but to afford a striking evidence of this position. The assumption of old theology is, that the Scriptures contain a revelation direct from the Supreme Deity, of a perfect rule of religious faith and practice; from this it follows that it must eventually be accepted by all people. Hence, in obedience to the command of their Master, to "go into all the world and preach the gospel to every creature," hundreds of pious men and women have gone; some with heroic devotion and self-sacrifice, others with sordid self-seeking, to carry this universal religion to the savage and barbarous nations of the earth. These enterprises have been liberally supported by the stated contributions of the pious, from the wealthy metropolitan church to the obscure parish of the rural districts. But the results have never been adequate to the efforts put forth. In fact it has been a magnificent failure—all statements in the monthly concerts of prayer for the heathen to the contrary notwithstanding. This position is so important, that I crave your indulgence while I substantiate it by some authorities, which will hardly be gainsaid by sectarians. The Rev. Justus Doolittle, for fourteen years a missionary of the American Board of Foreign Missions, in a work on China, says: "To make a single convert cost seven years' labor at Canton, and nine at Fuhschan; and it was twenty-eight years ere a church was organized. Out of four hundred million souls, there are as yet less than three thousand converts, as the result of the labors of two hundred missionaries, after sixty years of effort."

Sir Archibald Allison, a truthful historian, who, in comprehensive description, is second only to Macaulay, in his History of Europe says: "Great have been the efforts made, both by the Protestant and Roman Catholic churches, especially of late years, to diffuse the tenets of their respective faiths in heathen lands; but, with the exception of some Catholic missions of South America, without the success that was anticipated, at least in the outset Sectarian zeal has united with Christian philanthropy in forwarding the great undertaking; the British and Foreign Bible Society has rivaled in activity the propaganda of Rome, and the expenditure of £100,000 annually on the enlightenment of foreign lands has afforded a magnificent proof of devout zeal and British liberality. But no great or decisive effects have as yet followed these efforts; no new nations have been converted to Christianity; the conversion of a few tribes, of which much has been said, appears to be little more than nominal; and the durable spread of the gospel has been everywhere co-extensive only with that of the European race. The religion which obtains a lasting place in a country is often to be regarded as an effect rather than a cause. It is the consequence of a predisposition of the general mind which leads to the embracing of doctrines or forms."

But the successful conversion of the Sandwich Islanders has long been the stock in trade of the missionary zealot, in prompting the faithful to more liberal contributions to the missionary funds. But these sectarian pretensions are all corrected by the truthful statements of Mark Twain (Sam Clemens) that "forty years ago Hawaii contained two hundred thousand people—now about twenty thousand, and the population annually decreasing. There are three deaths to one birth. Thus we see nine-tenths have perished since the commencement of missions." These simple facts speak volumes in support of our position, and show that the kanakas, with all the sanctifying influences of this universal religion, like all savage people, when brought in close contact with civilized man, so take on his vices, without his moral stamina, as to surely dwindle towards practical extermination.

It is a further confirmation of this view that most nations while passing through a semi-civilized stage of unfoldment, should adopt the astronomical system of religion. It seems to be the natural order of the development of the human mind, when its powers of comprehension are enlarged, on beholding that the sun is far superior to any power located on earth—that it is the source from which emanate light and heat, which prompts the fertility of the soil, from which man draws his sustenance—that this incomprehensible power should become the object of religious worship. Accordingly we find that in the Egyptian valley of the Nile, the Persians on the plains about the Euphrates and the Tigris, the inhabitants of India, the Aztecs of Mexico, and the Incas of Peru, all adopted an almost identical system of religion, which consisted in worshiping the sun, the moon, and the starry firmament. These nations could scarcely have derived their religion one from the other, nor can it fairly be referred to an accidental coincidence, when we consider that the people of Mexico and Peru grew up in isolated positions, widely separated from all advanced nations, and wholly cut off from intercourse with any people advanced beyond the savage condition. So strong was this tendency among the Hebrews when they left Egypt, that to break it up Moses made it a capital offense to worship the sun, the moon, and the stars.

Another resultant of progression is this: that if, owing to those constant fluctuations, actions, and reactions, that constantly occur throughout every department of nature, the intellectual development of any people has outgrown the spiritual, a strong tendency to equilibrium will render a new spiritual growth inevitable. Such a condition of things exists at the present time. The spiritual growth of the civilized world is from one to two centuries behind the intellectual; and consequently religion is behind natural science, and the mechanic appliances to supply the external comforts of life. Hence we are in the midst of the throes of a transition period from a lower to a higher plane of spiritual unfoldment. This movement is the result of the all-pervading spiritual forces of our world. No power can arrest or stay its progress; it will carry humanity upon the ceaseless waves of spiritual progression towards the goal of more complete individualization of each, and the fraternal unity of all. By this intellectual development the powers of reason and criticism have become so increased that those evidences which, in the main, have satisfied previous generations of the great fact of a future life no longer suffice. And unless new evidence had been presented, which addressed itself to the reason and senses of every sincere and persevering investigator, the belief in a future life would gradually have faded from human consciousness.

But nature is true to herself. When this need was fully developed, the spiritual phenomena appeared as a general movement to supply such evidence of spirit life as is adapted to the intellectual requirements of the age.

It may be asked, Why did not spiritualism appear before? Why were those extraordinary manifestations reserved for the last half of the nineteenth century? If these questions were asked by an old theologian, I should answer, For the same reason that the revealments of Moses were not given to Adam or Noah, or Christianity to the Hebrew slaves of Egypt. If any other should ask these questions, I should answer, For the same reason that a period of which we can conceive no beginning passed before the matter composing our earth assumed the globular form; for the same reason that the earth pursued her annual journey around the sun for untold ages ere man made his appearance. It is fitting that the same century that has witnessed the general application of steam to mechanical labor—that has made the civilized world one network of railroads and telegraph lines; nay, it is fit that the decade which has spanned the deep valleys, the oozy plains, the rocky hills under the surging waters of the Atlantic, by a cable through which messages of intelligence, of affection, of joy, and perchance of sorrow, are transmitted with lightning speed, should also unfold to waiting humanity the relations of the spirit world and the law of spirit intercourse. True spiritualism is as old as humanity. So the diastole and systole motion of the heart propelled the blood in its ceaseless circuit through the veins, the capillaries, and the arteries of the human system before Harvey made that fact known to the scientific world. So the planets revolved about their primaries for countless ages before Copernicus, Kepler, Gallileo, and Newton revealed the facts and the laws to the human consciousness. History is replete with spiritual phenomena of which the text-books of the schools and all the systems of metaphysical philosophy which have succeeded and demolished each other from the days of Aristotle to Herbert Spencer afford no solution—nay, cast not a ray of light upon—which are all made plain to the comprehension of a child by spiritual facts and philosophy. Take the frequent occurrence of distinct impressions of the death of a near relative at a distance of hundreds of miles. Nothing is more natural than that a person dying, especially if separated from friends and relatives, should think, while passing the great changes, of the one he most loves, and should strongly desire the loved one's presence. As the spirit is separated from the body this desire becomes a motive power, carrying the perhaps scarcely conscious spirit with great rapidity till it impinges on the spirit of the loved one, imparting so much of its magnetism as to create the impression of the change through which the spirit of the relative has passed. Spiritualism renders this entire class of cases entirely plain, while every other system of mental philosophy leaves it in utter darkness.

Again; take the large class of cases of warnings of approaching danger. These abundant, well-authenticated cases are wholly inexplicable by any system of philosophy recorded in history anterior to the spiritual philosophy, which renders them as plain as any scientific fact. Stilling relates that Professor Bohm, teacher of mathematics at Marburg, while taking tea with company away from home, felt a sudden impulse to go home and remove his bed from the side of the room where it had stood, to another part of the room. Although no reason was given for it, the impression was so strong that he could have no peace until he went. He went home, had the bed removed, and returned to spend the remainder of the evening. That night about two o'clock he was awakened by a loud crash, when, on looking, he beheld a large beam, which had fallen, with part of the ceiling, lying across the spot from which he had removed his bed.

The following account I wrote down from the lips of the narrator, Henry Lewis, a truthful and reliable man: He was a pioneer in the early settlement of the town of La Grange, in northern Ohio. He had settled his family on a homestead covered with the original forest of beech, maple, hickory, oak, and other trees. He had formed a plan of felling several trees so as to throw the branches and trunks into a pile for burning, after the manner of woodmen, and commenced chopping the first tree. He was suddenly seized with an impulse to leave the tree. Although no reason was given for it, the impression was so strong that he went, but after considering that that was the tree to be felled first, returned to his labor. Again the impression seized him, stronger than before. Obedient to the mysterious impulse, he walked away again, when a large dry limb was loosened from its lodgment in the branches and came down whizzing through the foliage and struck directly in the tracks where he had stood, with sufficient force to have killed him instantly. These cases occurred long anterior to the modern manifestations, but if we admit the teaching of our beautiful faith—that we are attended through our earth life by guardian spirits attracted to us by affection; or to get that experience which an early death has denied them in the usual manner, and that these spirits, seeing clearer than we, and beholding the condition of their protégé, made extraordinary exertions to warn him of impending danger—and the solution of the mystery is complete.

In conclusion, allow me to make an obvious inference, that the human soul, being the highest product of nature's unfoldment, is in its essential essence pure and perfect; that its condition here is owing to those limitations, arrestments, and obstructions it has met with in the external conditions of its growth; and as all the improvements which have been made in the flowers that beautify the face of nature, and all the fruits and cereals that fill the land with abundance, have resulted from carefully studying nature's laws and methods and working with and assisting her, so it must be in the higher departments of morals and religion.

Let us not be deceived or disheartened at the apparently slow progress of humanity in substantial morality. Go look at the sun for five minutes and you cannot perceive that he has moved in his daily journey athwart the firmament; but remember that five minutes is, beyond comparison, longer, compared to a day, than the life of an individual is compared to the life of the race, which competent geologists estimate already to have been 100,000 years.

"Let us then be up and doing,
With a heart for any fate;
Still achieving, still pursuing,
Learn to labor and to wait."

As all things, from the vast to the minute, are continually progressing, we, too, must industriously push forward or inevitably be left in the rear.

"Nations may fall to rise no more,
Yet sounding on old Ocean's shore,
Amid the vast infinitude,
Is God's eternal interlude,
On!—forever on!"

THE COMING RELIGION.

A DRAMATIC ALLEGORY BY DR. JOHN ALLYN.

PUBLISHED 1882.

The "Vision of Aldeberan," on our first page, is recommended to the reader's attention as an interesting and a more than cursory glance in the direction of "The Coming Religion"—though it fails to present prominently one characteristic which must predominate in "the good time coming;" which is, the sentiment of Universal Brotherhood, or interest in and care for the welfare of each other. —*Banner of Light, September 9, 1882.*

[INTRODUCTION.—What is stated in this allegory in regard to its production is substantially true, though varied immaterially for the sake of brevity and interest. I have endeavored to put it in an attractive form, for even the diamond depends somewhat on its setting for the effect it may produce. If you do not approve of the setting, do not throw away the diamond. More than four months before a word was written I was assured that a band of spirits intended to make an important communication through my mediumship. This was written on a slate, in broad day, by no human hand, according to the most critical investigation—attested by my ears and my eyes. I had not the slightest idea what I could write. In fact, it seemed impossible that I could produce anything of value or interest. This was followed up for four months, through different mediums, all to the same import. I am not conscious of any desire to make money or fame out of this, but only hope it may benefit my fellow beings. I make this statement in regard to this extraordinary production because it is true, knowing that the matter contained in the article must stand on its intrinsic merit.—JOHN ALLYN.]

THE VISION OF ALDEBERAN.

Invocation:
    Guardian spirits, from danger defend us;
    In this imperfect state amend us;
    Help us to form a grand ideal,
    And strive to make its beauties real.
    So shall we walk life's dubious ways
    Until the dawn of brighter days.

Prelude:
    Friends of earth, we come to meet you,
    And most happy are to greet you;
    A happy band of teachers we,
    Two are men, and we are three.

    From far-off worlds we've come to teach
    Truths for earnest souls to preach;
    We've come to aid religion's birth,
    The last that e'er will come to earth,

    Give ear, kind friends, and listen well
    While we our wondrous story tell;
    A happy band of teachers we,
    Two are men, and we are three,
    The other is an angel pure,
    Whose kindly words will long endure.

On one of those delicious evenings of May, when it is a pleasure to be in the open air, as I was reclining on a bamboo lounge in front of my humble home, I queried if the stars which shone so beautifully were inhabited by beings of the human type; and if so, what the condition of society is in those various worlds. My mind was pained and oppressed at the condition of the children of the earth as I contemplated the wars, crimes of every grade, suicides, insanity, avoidable diseases and premature deaths; how some acquire vast fortunes in a few years, partly by superior energy and sagacity, partly by cunning, and often partly by fraudulent deceit, and spend their means in vulgar display, in foreign lands; while others, with haggard faces, work beyond their strength to gain the means of extending a wretched existence. Fatigued with these fruitless thoughts a tremor shook my frame, my senses were closed to external impressions, my mind was abnormally quickened, when the most ravishing music greeted my ear, the very thoughts

of which now thrill my soul with inexpressible delight.
The words I could not catch, but the chorus ran:

> From far-off worlds we've come to teach
> Truths for earnest souls to preach;
> We've come to aid religion's birth,
> The last that e'er will come to earth.

During this music three beings appeared before me, of surpassing beauty and perfection. For the first time my mind feasted in beholding human beings who were absolutely faultlessly perfect in feature, form, complexion, and expression, and beyond criticism by the most skillful artist. Two of these were men and one a woman. I intuitively perceived that their minds were as perfect as their physique appeared to be—not one faculty cultivated at the expense of another, nor the whole mind at the expense of the physical system.

One, whom for convenience I shall designate Dr. Symetricus Aldeberan, said: "We are an embassy from one of those stars you so admired as it twinkled beautifully in space." I suggested Alpha Centauri, sixty-one *cygni*. Aldeberan, with a majestic wave of his hand, he said: "It matters not; it is better you should not be informed, for the truths we have to utter must stand upon their own merits. We have some instruction to impart of great importance to the children of earth, and particularly to the American people. It has been our life-work, extending through æons and æons, to study the moral and religious growth of the people of the various planets as they have progressed from a savage condition to the highest and most perfect civilization.

"Of the six thousand stars you see twinkling so beautifully in the ethereal blue, some are binary, revolving about a common center; but the greater part are central suns with families of planets revolving about them, and receiving life-giving elements from their parent suns. The planets are in various stages of growth; some are in the diffused gaseous condition of irregular form, some are in the molten, fiery stage, and have, in obedience to attraction, assumed the globular form; some have radiated their heat until a crust is formed, the foundation of a peopled world. Some have reached the life-bearing stage, and in a small proportion life has progressed to the human type, while in a still smaller number, human beings and society have reached a condition inconceivably more perfect than on earth, while others have exhausted their life-bearing elements and become dead worlds, thus silently admonishing you of the fate of all worlds in the countless æons yet to come. As each aged person has passed through the various stages of infancy, early youth, later youth, manhood, maturer manhood, and so on to the stage of the decline of life's forces—so all planets have passed through the various stages described, or are on the inevitable road to those conditions.

"The reason that earth's inhabitants are in a disturbed and unhappy condition—that emperors are assassinated, vice, crime, and insanity are increasing in spite of increasing light, education, and power over the material resources of nature—is, that the people of earth are now passing through a religious transition period. The minds of the greatest thinkers are unsettled on the fundamental questions of man's origin, character, and destiny, from which practical morality springs; and there is said to be a moral interregnum. Your condition can be but little improved until this critical period in religion and morality is passed, and they become firmly established on the demonstrated truths and principles which inhere in the human constitution and its environment. The inhabitants of all worlds, older in development than yours, have passed through this same critical and disturbed period to one of greater harmony and happiness.

"We, whose business it is to be the teachers and helpers of our human brethren, have observed many worlds as they passed through this transitional period in religion and morals; we know its various stages and symptoms as well as a skillful physician knows the stages and symptoms of the most common disease. To make our meaning plain, we must premise that the people of all planets whose human race has reached a mature development have passed through three stages of religion; these are Fetichism, Polytheism, Monotheism, and so on to the Theanthropic, or the religion of humanity, which is the final and permanent condition. These are somewhat mixed and blended, as day vanishes through twilight to night, and night through rosy dawn, to full-orbed day. Fetichism is the religion of savage people; it consists in putting faith in inanimate objects, such as charms, trinkets, idols of wood and stone and metal; and in its highest expression consists, as by the Persians, in the worship of sun, moon, and stars. So fascinating was this, that Moses made it punishable with death, to wean the Hebrews from its practice. Polytheism consists in personifying the various forces of nature, and making a visible representation; thus, Jupiter flashed in the lightning, rolled in the thunder; Neptune controlled the ocean's storms. This found its culminating expression in Ephesus, Greece, and Rome, until their philosophers discovered its emptiness, and their satirists riddled it with ridicule, when it perished, never to appear again on earth. The Hebrew religion, as instituted by Moses, is an example of the purest Monotheism the world has ever seen.

"Christianity, its outgrowth, is a mixture of Monotheism, Polytheism, and Fetichism. Monotheism it receives from its progenitor. Its devil its trinity, especially its Christ, partake of the character of Polytheism. Its cross and sacred relics, and even its Bible, held so far above its intrinsic merit, partake of Fetichism. At the advent of Christianity, the cultured few in Greece and Rome saw the emptiness of their religion; but the masses were so sunk in ignorance and superstition, and so infatuated with their gods, that pure Monotheism could not have prevailed in Greece or Rome, or won its way over Odin and Thor in northwestern Europe. This mixture was a necessary condition of the success of Christianity. Most countries of distinctive civilization have originated their own religion. India originated Brahminism and Buddhism; Egypt had her Isis and Osiris; the Hebrews had their Jehovah; Greece had her gods; Scandinavia originated Odinism. Christianity was personal and local in its origin, adapted to a peculiar phase of civilization. Lord Beaconsfield thought the American people must be deficient in inventive faculties, or with a distinctive civilization they would have originated their own religion.

"He did not realize that a religion is now springing from the bosom of the American people that will be general in its character, supplanting all others and uniting them in religion as in government, education, and science."

I said: "Dr. Symetricus, you are aware that many of our thinkers, scientists, and philosophers think religion is unnecessary in civilized life. Will you please give us your views on that point?"

He replied: "This is a very important matter and

worthy our best consideration. If all were philosophers with well-cultivated moral faculties, society could exist without religion; but in reality we all commence our earthly life as children; and the worst of it is that, so far as our present argument is concerned, many of us remain children to the end of life. Very few attain to the power of clear reasoning on moral subjects until the age of twenty-five, and the majority of mankind do not during their natural lives. Conscience is an emotional power of the mind which, in its natural expression, affords no criterion of right or wrong. It simply enforces the convictions the mind has received through life's experiences and educational training; hence the importance that this training should be as efficient and correct as possible during early life while the mind is in its most plastic condition. This can only be effected through a religious system which can command the confidence of the scientists and philosophers of the country.

"It is necessary to the lucid treatment of a subject that its leading terms should be defined. This is especially true of religion, yet there is no adequate definition in your dictionaries; even your literary men are unable to give an adequate definition. The senior class of theological students of California cannot define it correctly; the lawyers of Philadelphia cannot; and, incredible as it may seem to a New Englander, even the transcendental philosophers of Boston and Concord cannot. Religion, according to its highest development, is a cult, whose object is moral culture as an end, and physical culture as a means to that end. According to the theology of the Middle Ages, which still lingers in the lap of the age of light; the objects of religion are to appease an angry God, to escape the wiles of a malignant devil, to escape a burning hell, to achieve some temporal good through prayer and observances, rather than by controlling the causes that lead to such blessings through the laws and forces that surround us.

"These ideas will be found to be myths having no foundation in reality and will be dropped from human consciousness as the people emerge into the latter part of this religious transition period."

I inquired what would become of religious worship.

He replied: "Worship has no effect whatever on the object or being worshiped, since everything that comes to us comes by, in, and through the laws of nature as they exist within our own being and environment. Worship may have a mild tendency to assimilate the worshiper to the object worshiped. We admit the Supreme Unitary Power of Nature, but still it must be plain that, in worshiping, a personal God is a pure ideal conception which every human being necessarily forms for himself. If this ideal be a 'man of war,' vengeful, angry at times, partial, elevating one tribe at the expense of exterminating others; punishing by endless torment the majority of his own creatures, the effect cannot but be demoralizing. The tendencies are partially counteracted by the wholesome moral tendency of all normally developed natures, by pleasant music, the eloquence of a cultured preacher, and the pleasant surroundings of a wealthy church. Worship, then, is a function of religion as transient in its character as animal sacrifice, and will not survive the present transition period."

I inquired what would be the first commandment in the new religion.

He replied: "The first commandment of the decalogue had a pertinent application to the people to whom it was given. Polytheism was the highest phase of religion which had obtained credence at that time. While Moses still lingered amid the smoke and thunderings of Sinai, the Hebrews clamored for a calf to worship, and Aaron yielded to their importunities. They had no doubt been educated to worship the sacred bull, Apis, of the Egyptians, an incarnation of the greater god, Osiris, in their mythology. Their early bias was so strong that they could not be satisfied without doing homage to an emblem of the god of their fathers.

"Moses undertook the difficult task of breaking up Polytheism and establishing the worship of the one God superior to all others, who was, in his system, the especial protector of the nation he essayed to establish; hence the pertinence of the first commandment, 'Thou shalt have no other gods before me.' But since, Polytheism has ceased to exist, for twelve centuries it has had no application whatever to the existing conditions of Christendom. During this time countless thousands have perished by living in violation of the plainest principles of physiology. This, then, should be the first command: *Thou shalt obey physiological law.*"

I inquired what doctrines of religion should be taught in regard to those great problems which are peculiarly religious—as the being and character of the Supreme Power of the Universe, the origin of man, the nature and destiny of the human spirit, and the relation of the spiritual world to the visible and material world we inhabit.

He replied: "The answer is very easy, and very plain. That which is known and can be verified should be taught; that which is not known should be investigated. It is the same rule which obtains in science, in agriculture, in mechanics In all of these a working hypothesis is useful in investigation as a ground of experiment, and these have led to some of the most important discoveries in science. But there is a clear distinction between these provisional assumptions and demonstrable truths. But henceforth the mind must be left free; let no religious teachers and no ecclesiastical councils attempt to trammel the human mind; let them not say you must believe this or you must not believe that under penalty. Belief is involuntary; it is the conclusion of the intellect from the evidence as the mind sees it.

"Original and free investigation for an honest purpose is as commendable in religion as in science. It is the primary duty of religious teachers, as a class, to enlarge the boundaries of human knowledge in regard to these great matters. If this rule be observed—preach what is known, search out what is unknown—you will not be troubled with long sermons on hot afternoons as many have been in the days of their youth.

"Religious exercises must mainly be addressed to the emotions; for all are emotional, whether young or old, learned or unlearned. But the doctrinal teaching must not be offensive to the few who have cultivated the reasoning faculties to the highest degree and are the best posted in scientific matters. Poetry, eloquence, and music must ever remain the fit instruments of religious exercises."

I inquired of my teacher what he thought of our public schools as a means of moral improvement.

He laughed at the idea. "We thought so at one time on our planet, but that was æons and æons ago when our schools were in a similar condition to yours at the present time. A singular circumstance happened which brought to light a fact not mentioned in our current histories. An autiquarian who spends his life in hunting for scraps of forgotten lore, in searching among the voluminous archives found an ancient document which appeared well authenticated with the seal of a great and proud State, which showed that in those remote times teachers actually resorted to fraud to gain certificates of their qualifications for teachers. This seemed incredible to our people; but it was further shown that neither moral nor religious principles were taught. Little or no training was given to fit the pupils for the actual business of life, nor was it impressed on them that all necessary labor is honorable. On the contrary, some teachers told their pupils that education was a means of sharpening the faculties so they could escape their share of labor. Then it began to dawn on the people that their public-school system was inadequate to the work in hand of properly training the young.

"As our planet passed the last religious transition, moral and religious instruction went hand in hand with secular education; and what may seem incredible to you, the religious teaching took hold of the minds of the young, because it corresponded with the laws of nature and was verified and confirmed by all subsequent experience. We no longer heard the alarming remark that crime and vice increased with increasing intelligence. And no education is considered complete which does not enable the recipient to observe closely, reason accurately, analyze completely, and educe a correct conclusion on any subject, in spite of the ordinary bias of passion, prejudice, and preconceived opinion; also, all training of the young had special reference to fitting them for the places they were most likely to occupy in mature life.

"In the coming religion man will rise into the region of causes and fully appreciate their relative and absolute power in every department of affairs; and the fruitlessness of all efforts for improvement which dabble with effects alone. Within the last half-century man has made wonderful strides in obtaining a mastery over the forces and materials of nature. Continents have been gridironed with steel rails and telegraph wires, and machinery has been applied to manufacture everything requisite to his comfort. It now remains for man to gain the mastery over himself, as an individual, and as a race composed of the aggregate of individuals. He must rise to a clear perception of the causes which lead to such a normal development of the physical, intellectual, and moral powers as shall render easy and habitual the obedience to physiological requirements for the highest development of the individual and of the race. Then diseases will almost cease to afflict, and medicines will literally and figuratively become a drug in the market. Excessive wealth and excessive poverty, will alike cease. Wealth will be no excuse for idleness nor poverty for overwork. The new religion will be a powerful and indispensable auxiliary in producing these results. The requisite principles will be taught from childhood and enforced by the moral power of example."

I inquired of my venerable instructor how his physiological principles should be put into practice.

He answered: "There was a time in the history of our planet when it presented great difficulties on account of interested professionals and the vulgar prejudices of uncultured and undeveloped minds; but as our people began to emerge from the age of faith and mythology to the age of scientific religion, a sanitary commission was established by law and supported by the State.

"This consisted of three for every ten thousand, whose lives were devoted to physiological studies. All candidates for matrimony were required to be examined by this commission, somewhat as an applicant for life insurance has to be with you.

"A careful record of this was kept in the archives of State to be held private for the uses intended. If the applicants misrepresented they were liable to the penalties of perjury; if, contrary to instruction, they became parents and were afflicted with children of a feeble and sickly constitution, doomed to an early death or sickly life; they could not lay the blame to a mysterious providence or expect the sympathy of their neighbors and friends. Common sense, foresight, and prudence all contributed to work out a glorious result. In a few generations the children were uniformly strong, healthy, and beautiful, and it was a great source of pleasure to look at them and witness their sports.

"Say not that such a discrimination will be dishonorable or disreputable to that moiety who are assigned other duties and other pleasures than those of parentage. These crude ideas spring from undeveloped brains, the result of semi-civilized conditions.

"The dishonorable part is to hand down to innocent and helpless generations of the future evils which foresight, wisdom, and the exalted morality we teach might avoid.

"There can be no greater misery than to become parents of children of sickly and feeble constitutions, inevitably doomed to early death, or, worse still, to drag out a life alike joyless to themselves and useless to the society in which they dwell; nor can there be a more keen and poignant suffering than the stings of conscience to a sensitive soul when evils result from a violation of the best religious instruction the world has ever seen. Darwin has demonstrated to the scientific world that animal life has attained its present status through the operation of the laws of heredity, variation, natural selection, and the survival of the fittest. Humanity must be carried up to a still higher plane through the same laws, with the addition of physiological and moral selection. Let no one say that we teach the hideous doctrine of free love. On the contrary, we teach the absolute sacredness of true marriage, and that the highest expression of love should be chastened and directed by the highest wisdom and most exalted morality. Those who are unfit to become parents by physiological conditions are entitled to a joyous and happy existence; as much so as their natural constitutions and circumstances will permit; but the most serene and soulful happiness is impossible to those who are not truly useful to the society in which they live and the human race as as a whole."

He continued: "When people learn to live according to physiological requirements and conditions, medicines will be but little needed. The medical profession will be more useful, even, than it is now. It will be elevated from writing Latin prescriptions for drugs of doubtful utility to pointing out in plain English sanitary laws and conditions, which will result in avoiding the greater portion of the diseases that afflict humanity. A constitutional vigor will be developed which will enable each one to resist slight unwholesome conditions which cannot be avoided in the present condition of your planet. But as your planet progresses to the mature condition of the human bearing period; the meteorological, electrical, magnetic, and other sanitary conditions will be greatly improved. This, in connection with voluntary efforts on the part of the people, will carry humanity up to a condition of happiness and perfection beyond the most poetic dreams of the Utopian philosophers."

I inquired what would be the result of the apparent antagonism between labor and capital.

He replied: "These agitations and disturbances will cease as society becomes elevated by the operation of the forces we have named. When the new religion becomes firmly and fully established, by its code of moral ethics, no one will be permitted to perform more than six hours of earnest, taxing labor in a day, either of the brain or muscles; and this for various reasons: 1st. It will be ample to provide for all the wants of mankind and accumulate a generous surplus for any exigency that may arise. 2d. For any man to perform more than six hours of muscular labor a day will deteriorate the brain and so invite immoralities that will do society far more evil than the surplus labor will benefit; and, also, more than six hours of brain labor will deteriorate the muscular system, disturbing the symmetry and harmony of every part of the system, thus disturbing conditions necessary to the best intellectual efforts. There will then be little or no labor that is not also a pleasure. To a great extent every one will be permitted to choose his own occupation and pursue it with interest. The distinction between amateur and professional work will cease. Every one will be ambitious to excel in his or her efforts, and sham, make-shift work will afflict the world no more. The idea should be taught from early years and brought to the consciousness of the people, that all children are the wards of the State to a certain extent, for on them the welfare of the future nation mainly depends. And the State should most imperatively be required to furnish medical advice to all who are raising families I have observed with pain that in some towns it requires the wages of two days' common labor to pay for one doctor's visit and medicines. Think for a moment of a young man and woman of little means struggling to rear children under such conditions! If Jupiter still controlled the thunder and had a particle of sense of justice, he would make the lightnings flash and the thunders roll, as if all the artillery of the world were exploding, until such wrongs were abated.

"One of the principles of the ethical code of the new religion will be, that population must resolutely be kept within the means of proper subsistence. The maxim of one of your great political economists, that there is a constant tendency of population to outrun the means of subsistence, does not hold good where reason and the moral element are so trained as to induce right living, unswayed by passion or prejudice. The present idea that a rapid increase of population is desirable is the offspring of avaricious greed. The newspaper man, the professional man, the merchant, and the railroad man all desire customers which a greater population may bring; hence false ideas of political economy have become common, and habits of life naturally follow quite inconsistent with the highest prosperity and moral development of the people. It must be kept in mind, that in a true condition of society a larger proportion of productive wealth must be spent in education and recreative enjoyments."

He continued: "I have observed with pain that in every city there are hundreds, and in small towns scores, of men and women dragging out miserable lives of feebleness and ill-health because their fathers and mothers—good, pious souls!—robbed their unborn children of their inherent patrimony of constitutional vigor by overwork, through an unwise ambition to keep up a certain style of living or to accumulate property. They attended church services regularly, but heard no word of warning from their pastor; verily, as the Hebrew prophet said three thousand years ago, they were dumb dogs that could not bark. They employed physicians and paid them liberally for Latin prescriptions, but received no adequate warning from them in matters of most vital importance. Under the new religion, the mothers of the race will be treated more tenderly than they have been; especially by the struggling classes. The people will be religiously bound to place them in happy surroundings, favorable to poetic, artistic, and intellectual exaltation, and most conscientiously to exempt them from all burdensome labor of body or mind, that they may give their strength to their children; for no education, no preaching, no medical treatment, no prisons or scaffolds can compensate for antenatal losses and misdirection."

I asked the doctor what he thought of the climate of the United States.

Said he: "Here is a matter worthy of careful consideration. Owing to the electrical, magnetic, and other subtle conditions not understood, there is a tendency to an undue development of the nervous system. This is seen in the ominous precocity and thin muscles of children and the increase of nervous diseases. These causes are powerful and not easily controlled. The American continent has been the graveyard of nations. The Mound-builders have passed away and left no record but the earthworks they built for some scarcely defined object. If there is no counteracting cause or balance-wheel introduced to correct this tendency, when the fresh currents of European blood cease to be poured into the veins of the people, they will become a nation of invalids. The only adequate remedy is to drive home physiological principles by the powerful means of religious teaching.

"When there is a lively and sensitive conscience developed in this matter, aided by such discoveries as our scientists shall make, man will here, as elsewhere, gain a glorious triumph over the obstacles which nature seems to have thrown in his way."

I asked my venerated instructor if he would be pleased to give his views of Colonel Ingersoll and his work.

He replied: "Most willingly. His career is an index of the times of great significance. He is doing a splendid work of a preliminary character. He is an iconoclast breaking the images the people have been so long worshiping. He is blessed with great eloquence, great personal magnetism, great talent for producing immediate results, but there is not an element of reconstructive force in his nature. His reputation will be short-lived, for no man ever did a great and lasting work on a mere negation. His religion of good dinners and good clothes does not fill the diapason of human emotions, human fears, and human hopes. Such a man could only find his mission in the early part of this transition period, when thousands of men and women have severed their connection with the decaying religion of the past and have not yet reached out their tendrils to find support in the far better religion of the future. He describes with unfaltering audacity the thoughts that have long had their silent undergrowth, but, from an excusable timidity, have shrunk from the light of day. As my colleague will explain, the evolution system has cut the tap-root of Mediæval Theology, and Colonel Ingersoll is working with herculean strength to sever the roots that spread upon the surface. His work is to clear the ground of the rubbish and obstruction which are no longer either useful or ornamental. Others of equally great talents, eloquence, and personal magnetism will take up the work where he leaves it; they will drive the plowshare deep through the virgin soil; angels will sow the pure seed, which will spring up with a vigorous growth and produce a bounteous crop for the healing and nourishing of countless generations yet to be."

SISTER ALDEBERAN'S ADDRESS.

"Oh, my sisters of earth! permit me to address you a few sisterly words. Could you be permitted to behold our transcendent beauty by the clear perception of the inner mind, as your speaker has done, it would excite your rapturous admiration; ay, perchance your envy, for we are all human. This beauty and physical perfection is not a chance gift, but has come through the operation of natural laws and forces which are omnipresent. True, it was our good fortune to have been born and reared in a planet which had reached the maturity of its life-bearing forces; still we are indebted to a long line of ancestors of both sexes who had religiously obeyed the laws of health, without which such beneficent results were impossible. The past cannot be recalled, but the future of earth is all before you; permit me, therefore, to address you a few sisterly suggestions; for, though I never suffered a day of painful illness or conscious physical weakness, yet through the subtle sympathy of sex I can appreciate the evils that have afflicted you, oh, sisters of earth! Resolve now to begin to study and obey the laws of health, which will in time work out inconceivable results to a grateful posterity.

"Not to be too vague and general, let me descend to a few salient particulars: Never allow your clothing to press so closely on any part of your person as in the slightest degree to impede the circulation of the blood and the subtle nerve-nourishing elements it carries. Remember that any pressure on either of the four extremities, by an inevitable reaction, also impedes the healthful nutrition of the brain, thus incapacitating it to put forth the most perfect emotions and ideas.

"But, above all, avoid any pressure on the vital organs

that may fetter the heart-throbs which send the nourishing currents to every part of the system or which may prevent the full inflation of the lungs, by which that current is oxygenated with the life-giving elements of the atmosphere.

"All wrongs of this kind are avenged by nerve and brain deterioration and all its attendant aches and evils. These suggestions may seem trivial, but they are not so; for due attention to them, with appropriate open-air life, will enable the oxygen to paint your complexion beyond the picture of the most skillful artist. It will also give to your nerves a pleasurable sense of existence which all the medicines of the world cannot approach. Try to develop a reasoning brain and an independent character. In early life acquire skill in some useful industry that will help to give you a sense of independence and be a refuge in adversity.

"In the planet I represent, what is accepted as the most perfect model of the female form is slightly fuller in the chest and waist than your justly celebrated statue of *Venus de Medici*. After mature consideration by our best physiologists, it was concluded that anything more restricted would not give the vital organs sufficient strength to sustain the highest beauty and meet the inevitable exigences of life; and hence statues of this model are placed in many public places, and even in some of our religious edifices; not as the vulgar may suppose, to worship, but as a means of culturing a correct public taste.

"We are alive to the great fact that the healthful manifestations of the affections are the crowning glory of a woman in all worlds; but still I am impelled to say even the sacred affections should be dominated, directed, and controlled by that superior wisdom which can only come of a healthful physique and the careful training of self-discipline.

"Accept these sisterly admonitions in the kindly spirit in which they are given, and you and posterity will have occasion to hold me in grateful remembrance.

"And, oh, my sisters! allow me in conclusion to say the most important word of all, which may appear extravagant; but weigh it well before you pronounce it so.

"As to be the mother of a child, healthy and sound of body and mind is the greatest crown of glory to a woman, so to bear a sickly one is the greatest sin. Therefore firmly resolve that, unavoidable exigences excepted, you will never bear a sickly, feeble child. Struggle to carry out this heaven-born resolution, even to death, knowing that if you fall in so holy a cause you will fill an enviable niche among the martyred saints in the great temple of the future religion of humanity.

"In the Christian religion God was said to be manifested in the flesh of one man. It is the aim of this religion that He should be manifest in every human being."

DR. INTUITUS' ADDRESS.

I said, Dr. Intuitus, what do you think of the materialization phenomena?

A dark shade of sorrow spread over his expressive features as he replied: "In time they will be perfected, but at present they are in a very unsatisfactory condition. We are dependent mainly on these phenomena to convince the scientists and materialists of the continuance of intellectual life, after the change of death. Those who have charge of this department in spirit life find it exceedingly difficult to control the delicate conditions necessary to produce the best possible results. Mediums seem to be wanting in proper training or destitute of some qualities requisite to complete success in this matter; and yet it is very difficult to treat the subject properly. To mediumship, conscious and unconscious, the world is mainly indebted for progressive impulses and powers to lift it to a higher plane, not only in religion and morals, but also to some extent in mechanical inventions.

"Mediumship is surrounded by such subtle and delicate forces, and is manifested in such a variety of phases that it is very imperfectly understood by the mediums themselves, much less by the world at large. The rule holds good here that it is better that a hundred guilty parties escape than that one innocent should suffer; and yet it is painfully true that unscrupulous men, from mercenary motives, have taken advantage of the strong desire on the part of the people to see a palpable demonstration of a future life to perpetrate shameful frauds. These things impose the necessity of learning to discriminate between the worthy and the unworthy, the true and the false. Every banker is compelled to learn to discriminate between genuine money and its counterfeit; and the government is bound to ferret out the guilty parties in order to protect the people. In our planet a class of professional experts grew up to detect and expose such frauds. Persons were treated with delicate consideration while there was a doubt of the character of the medium or his effort. But when a man was found to perpetrate an unscrupulous fraud, simulating so holy and useful a power, they would put a whip in the hands of every honest man to *lash the rascal naked through the world.*"

I said, Dr. Intuitus, as you have some reputation for being clairvoyant and prophetic, will you tell us how long the transition period will continue?

He replied: "You are in the early part of the period. By the end of this century the scientists will have mastered the spiritual phenomena and explained their import; or at least they will have so raised the vail of darkness and mystery that seems to enshroud them that progress will be pleasant and rapid. By the middle of the next century the transition will be passed and the new religion fully established; for the human mind is so ripened and cultured that more progress is now made in fifty years than was in three centuries at the advent of the Christian era. Then people will look back on the grand old city churches as we look on the ruins of the ancient temples of Thebes, Ephesus, and Greece, as mementos of a faith, once powerful, but now departed from the earth—with a few exceptions — mostly in some inaccessible mountain region, remote from the centers of population and thought. And as I see some pious souls weeping over these stately ruins, I say, 'Weep not, oh children of earth; the evolution that has destroyed these will build edifices of far more value to mankind. Weep not; a religion that could fruit in the Crusades, the Massacre of St. Bartholomew, the Thirty Years' War, the horrors of the Inquisition, a personal devil, and an endless hell of burning fire, is not worthy of your tears.'

When the true history of this transition is written, it will be seen that men and women have lived and labored on American soil, of a higher inspiration, and a deeper spiritual insight than any priest or prophet that ever trod the sacred soil of Palestine; or any evangelist that wrote the sayings or doings of Jesus Christ; or any apostle who carried the religion of a blood-atonement to the heathen nations of the earth.

"I will now explain more in detail. The Reformation

of the sixteenth century may be considered as the first indication of the approaching change. The reformers started with the principle of the right of private judgment, but practically crippled its effect by limiting it to their own book and creed. If any one in the exercise of his judgment transcended these limits he was anathema maranatha. Protestantism, therefore, being but a half-work, has been a sickly failure; bearing the seeds of contradiction and decay in its own bosom, it was foredoomed to a short life. The Augsburg and Westminster confessions of faith completely arrested further progress and growth in religious knowledge, and they will remain in history as sad mementos of the danger of fixing human belief and investigation. During the last third of a century, which may fairly include the transition period, two grand achievements have been made: One is the ability to command at will the scientific evidence of a continued existence after the dissolution of the mortal body. What has already appeared are as the pattering drops that often precede a copious shower. As these phenomena are in a state of rapid development, I will not further dwell upon them here.

"The other is the grandest achievement the inhabitants of earth have ever made—I mean the establishment of the universal doctrine of Evolution. This great work has been done mainly by the English and American scientists. For the last third of a century many men whose intellects have never been excelled, have worked with great and persistent industry.

"They have examined mountains, deserts, continents, and seas; they have peered through telescopes and microscopes; they have chipped away with the geologist's hammer at the solid crust of the earth; they have examined scientifically all the known forms of living and extinct animal life; some of the greatest intellects have examined, compared, and analyzed the facts so obtained. Out of all this has at length sprung the doctrine of Universal Evolution, as the principle by which all things exist. It explains the origin of worlds, the origin and growth of animal life, of governments, religions, systems of philosphy, and everything pertaining to human beings and conditions. This universal solvent, the key-note of the universe; has at length, in spite of much learned and religious opposition, won its way to scientific recognition. It is now taught in most colleges and universities, and is heartily accepted by all whose departments pertain to biological science. This bringing into light the eternal verities of the evolution system has cut the tap-root of Middle-Age theology by showing how man has attained his present status without the intervention of special acts of creation, or special providences. It has also indicated how a religious system can be evolved that will be based on truths that can be verified scientifically. We should by no means despise the past or passing religions; they are the best the world was capable of at the time of their advent, and were necessary stages of the world's progress. As well may the new-hatched chick despise the egg—a homogeneous mass of albuminoid matter inclosing the yolk, and itself kept in position by a thin, porous shell of carbonate of lime. But in the course of incubation there comes a time when the shell is no longer useful, but must be got rid of or progressive growth will be thwarted.

"Now comes the next stage. During the remainder of this century the spiritual phenomena will be examined, elucidated, and explained, and their relation to other sciences established. Already two English scientists—Wallace and Crookes, both Fellows of the Royal Society, itself a guaranty of scientific eminence—have made a good beginning in elucidating these phenomena. Frederick Zöllner, Professor of Astronomy in the University of Leipsic, has written a book in which he has endeavered to show that there is a fourth dimension of space in which spiritual beings exist, wholly inappreciable to our senses. These works cannot but arouse many to this great theme. For this work we must depend on our young men who have a life-work to choose and a reputation to achieve. Most of the older scientists have devoted themselves so absorbingly to the great work of elucidating the evolution theory through that moiety of science that addresses itself to the external senses; that they have allowed their faculties of spiritual discernment to become inactive and dormant. Huxley, perhaps the greatest living naturalist, said, 'Even if the spiritual phenomena are true, they do not interest me.' Probably not; for, notwithstanding his great learning and ability, he can no more comprehend the contents of the fourth dimension, than an unlettered peasant can appreciate the principles of the evolution system he has so beautifully illustrated. Others of equally great abilities and industry will take hold of this work, and by the end of this century the greatest achievement of the ages will be established — the relation of the spiritual beings of the fourth dimension to those still in the flesh made palpable; and materialism forever banished from the earth. Then will the scientists perceive the truth and beauty of the saying of one of earth's greatest poets, 'There are more things in heaven and earth than are dreamed of in your philosophy.'

"At the commencement of the next century, having gained over the scientists, philosophers, and unbiased literary men, the effective brain-power of any people, from this coign of advantage the hosts of liberal spiritualism will go forth to do valiant battle with the obstructive power of Middle-Age theology; conscious of a final victory. The principal strength of an obstructive theology lies in its wealth. Vast amounts have been invested in church edifices and theological schools, and on your earth money is power. Money-making men of no more spiritual discernment than the golden god they worship, will continue to give to sustain this moribund religion. Like most other lights of the church, they can see what is, but cannot discern the far more glorious temples yet to be in the coming religion of humanity. They repeat, parrot-like, Paul's saying, 'The things that are seen are temporal, but the things that are unseen are eternal,' and know nothing of its tremendous power and import. The new religion, having passed the middle of the transition period, will have gained such a power of momentum that nothing can resist it.

"People will look back in amazement that a religion, based neither on fact, philosophy, nor practical morality, could have prevailed so many centuries after the human mind became awake to scientific progress, mechanical invention, and industrial enterprise. It was not founded upon a fact, but on the myth that its founder was a supernatural being (begotten by the third person of the trinity), a myth so easily claimed, so impossible of proof. Not founded on philosophy, because it claims to be proved by miracles, thus flying in the very teeth of the uniformity of nature's laws and processes — the principle that renders science possible and valuable; not based upon practical morality, because the vilest murderer, who sends his victim — with all his sins unannealed — to endless torment, may himself go directly to a heaven of endless happiness by the mere profession of faith in this religion.

"The great work of both philosophers and philanthropists is, to rid the world of the terrible incubus of a religion that has stood in square opposition to science through all these centuries of human progress, and trembled at every important achievement.

"After the advent of the twentieth century the teachers of mediæval theology will cease to be respected. Men of talents will avoid the profession, and men of inferior caliber can only present a feeble barrier to stay the rising tide of human progress. When the people see how they have been misled and deceived, the accumulated wrongs of centuries of false teachings, will burst forth in a storm of uncontrollable indignation toward the clergy which will overstep the bounds of propriety. The capacity of the English language will be taxed to the utmost in invective, sarcasm, and denunciation. They will openly accuse them of moral and intellectual prostitution. They will refuse to be appeased until the teachers of the coming religion show them that the clergy themselves, as well as the people, are the victims of a false religion, which originated in the undeveloped condition of the human mind in the barbarous ages of the distant past.

"I see in the distance a grand struggle for the American people, such as the world has never seen—one that will involve the question of the life and death of republican liberty. Many will be forced to take positions which were at first distasteful to them—even as they have had to in struggles already past. I do not propose to discuss this topic in detail in this lecture, reserving it for a future address. Suffice it to say that the struggle will not be short, but sharp and terribly decisive. A power that has no business on the American continent, as a power wielded by a foreign potentate, will be crushed forever by the hosts of human liberty. The votaries of this power are far-seeing, eager, confident of success; exceedingly fond of power and possessed of the best religious organization the world has ever seen for the accumulation and conservation of power. And be assured they aim at nothing less than the entire subjugation of the American republic to their uses and purposes. While they are determined and steady in their aim; the others, though greatly in the majority, are indeterminate, scattered, antagonistic, and totally destitute of a well-grounded religious polity—and seem likely to remain with a ruinous indifference until the horrors of the impending conflict drive them to an appreciation of the circumstances that surround them, and the dangers that threaten them. As these things progress, the inherent weakness of Protestantism becomes apparent. It becomes so plain that the densest mind can no longer ignore the potent fact that the Bible on which it is founded, being full of errors, was simply the product of the human intellect, like other books.

"They are compelled to perceive that there are but two sides in this conflict; that they must go back and join the power from which their forefathers parted, or go forward and join the hosts of progressive liberty. Some from conservative motives, will go back, but will lie uneasily in their chosen bed.

"When the people have taken sides there will come a time when it must be decided which power will control this government; a long-impending crisis will at length come, and as has happened before, the party in the wrong will throw down the gage of battle, and the other party will be forced to take it up or submit ignominiously to lose everything that makes life valuable. As heretofore, the hosts of darkness will gain some important victories; this will only serve to unite firmly the hosts of liberty—they will fear that history may repeat itself; the shrieks of the victims of St. Bartholomew will pierce their ears, and they will hear the clanking of the implements of the Inquisition. Then the tide of battle will turn, and every move will hasten and compel the total destruction of the great obstructive power on the American continent. When the victory is won and the smoke of the conflict clears away, it will be seen that the new religion and the new state will interblend their harmonious forces like my fingers, one supporting the others.

"Then it will be perceived that true religion is something more than an abstraction; that on earth it requires an institution to express itself through, even as a spirit requires a body; that it is a living, vital force, indispensable to conserve the morals necessary to sound government and wholesome society. The new religion having triumphed over its foes, outgrown its childish weaknesses, and petty sects, humanity will enter on its long millennium of prosperity and happiness beyond the power of the present generation to conceive. So great will be the improvement of society that war will cease, prisons will be changed into manufactories, and asylums to palaces of arts and scientific research. Here and there a church may be found of those who think that Adam and Eve were created perfect, and the golden age lies in the distant past; these will linger like winter in the lap of spring, or a glacier pushed down to the very verge of the fruiting vineyards."

Experience with Spirits
—for a—
Quarter of a Century.

On the first of October, 1860, I landed in New York from nearly a month's sea voyage, including the Isthmus transit. Those who have not experienced something of the kind, can scarcely realize the pleasure and mental exhilaration felt, after being pent up in a crowded ship for twenty days, on reaching one's native shore. So boisterous was the expression of this in songs, jokes, laughter, and the like, on the night preceding the landing that sleep was impossible. For nine years I had led a rough life in California, banished from the pleasures of what in older communities we call society.

I had a strong desire to investigate for myself the phenomena of modern spiritualism. I had seen nothing but table-tipping, which was unsatisfactory because it was difficult to determine how much unconscious muscular action and cerebration, might be mixed with the psychic force in producing the results seen.

I landed on Saturday, and on Sunday I attended a spiritual lecture, at the close of which it was announced that there would be a seance the next evening, naming the street and number. I was an entire stranger to nearly every person in the city, and on inquiring if strangers were admitted was told they were on payment of twenty-five cents. According to intention I went, not expecting to participate further than to be a looker-on. I found about a dozen men and women sitting around an extension dining-table in a double parlor; others were sitting about the room. The medium, Mrs. Malone, was sitting at the end of the table.

I took a seat at the table; soon the medium became entranced and seemed to personate some one dying of consumption—seemed to have a hacking cough and was distressed for breath. This was wholly novel to me, but seemed not to be to others; some lowered the window to relieve the distress of the medium, while one and another inquired, " Is it my spirit friend?" About a year before, a brother had, in common parlance, died, and also ten years previous another. As was natural, my mind was fixed on the one who had died recently.

To all other inquiries the medium shook her head and motioned her hand toward me. I arose and took it and inquired, "Is this George?" She shook her head and took her watch out of her belt, and laying it in her left hand pointed to it with her right forefinger. I thought I detected brother Matthew's expression of features on her face, but of this I might be mistaken. But as he had been a jeweler and worked with watches, the watch feat convinced me and I said, This is Matthew. She nodded assent. I then addressed him and said: " Have you anything further you wish to communicate?" The medium took a pencil and paper and wrote, "I have exhausted the medium in making myself known; at another time I will answer all your questions."

When a miner strikes the color or a few cents to the pan, he follows it up hoping to find a rich lead; accordingly I called on the medium the next day, and she passed into a trance and I conversed for an hour with that brother, as if face to face, talking of matters pertaining to our previous life unknown to any person in the city. I inquired how spirit life compared with the earth life? He said it was far superior and inexpressibly glorious, but it was impossible for him to give me an adequate idea of it then. I have since thought that some unhappy circumstances of his earth life may have had something to do with his feeling in estimating the two conditions. To say that I was convinced of the fact of spirit existence and communion and was greatly delighted, is but a feeble expression of my state of mind.

A. E. Horton, of San Diego, whose acquaintance I made at the hotel where I was stopping, told me of a man who was an excellent writing medium, who gave seances every week at his house as an amateur, and made no charge for his services, and offered to introduce me to him without giving my name so as to help to get a test. I gladly accepted the offer. I found him a plain man of about fifty, who worked a farm in the vicinity. At the sitting, among others he wrote a letter addressed to me, and signed the name of the aforementioned brother, Matthew Allyn. This letter was in a handwriting that resembled that of my brother, but in a marked degree the idiomatic expressions were his, and also capital letters were used oftener than is common, which was a habit with him. I kept the letter ten years, and then, at her request, sent it to his oldest daughter, then married to Thomas Ogden of Wellington, Ohio.

The spirits urged me to engage in lecturing, to promulgate the fact and philosophy of spirit intercourse with mortals. After visiting my friends in Ohio I did so, giving some twenty lectures, wading through snow, mud, and sleet to fill my appointments. Twenty years later on visiting that part of the country I found some good spiritualists as fruits of my humble and unsupported labors. The premonitory mutterings of the civil war were then thick in the air, and I reluctantly concluded that the public mind was too much excited with approaching troubles to be easily interested in supra-mundane affairs. My labors and exposure to a climate more severe than I had been accustomed to caused a severe sickness, in the spring while in New York.

AN APPARITION AND WHAT CAME OF IT.

In March, 1861, I went to Dr. Jackson's water cure near Dansville, in western New York. I came to the conclusion that I must soon return to California. Six months had passed and I had met with no one who seemed quite adapted to be my companion for the balance of life's journey. I was about to turn my back upon every relative I had in the world and put the Rocky mountains and two thousand miles between me and them. I realized what every intelligent person must know, that at that period California was a poor place to find a wife. I felt lonely and sad. It seemed that a crisis in my fate had arrived, and I felt that it was not good to be alone. At this time the apparition of a lady appeared dressed in Quaker drab. I knew not either the cause or significance of this visitor. I soon went to New York city with its half a million, with scarce an exception strangers to me. I soon met the lady represented by said vision and knew her on sight. We were married, and on our way to California early in June, while the soldiers were gathering for the great struggle for union and liberty.

WHAT OCCURRED ON THE PASSAGE.

Contrary to my expectations, the steamer was crowded with about a thousand passengers, some fleeing from impending trouble. On the passage I made the acquaintance of Victor Smith, a fellow-passenger, with a commission in his pocket as Collector of Customs for Puget Sound district. I told him I had spent several years there and knew something of the climate, country, and people. He said the authorities wished to ascertain what the actual cost of keeping the patients at the Marine Hospital was. They had been kept on contract at a dollar and a half a day each, and he thought there was a great profit at that. He said that it was necessary to let the contract at a fixed sum, with a verbal agreement to return to the government all but a fixed salary. He wished to find some reliable man to undertake this. Before the end of our voyage he offered me the position which I accepted, and faithfully carried out the project, and returned in one year over four thousand dollars to the government in its time of sore need. My position was no sinecure; in fact, the care and labor were too much for my slender constitution, and for this and other causes I left at the expiration of the terms of the contract, and went to Victoria to improve some property I had there. I continued until the winter of 1864 when it seemed necessary to find a place on American soil for permanent settlement. I had some doubt whether to go to Seattle, then a mere hamlet in the wilderness; or to Oakland, California, a suburb of San Francisco, of two thousand inhabitants. Again my spirit friends came to my assistance and decided the matter by this couplet:

> "Make your home under the oak tree's shade
> And not under that by the pine-tree made."

I did so. Oakland grew rapidly, and my little investment proved a small bonanza which has since been a refuge and solace.

The question may arise here, Will spirits help us to make money? My experience and observation lead me to the conclusion that if our motives are pure, and we desire means to enable us to do good, we may attract a highly developed class of spirits who may help us to accumulate property; but if our motives are simply to aggrandize ourselves and outshine our neighbors, the class of spirits we will attract may mislead us to serious loss. I could give many instances to illustrate this.

SLATE-WRITING.

For eight years I have occasionally had slate writings by some force unknown to science, signed by some spirit friend. The best were had this year by the mediumship of Mrs. C. L. Reid, between two slates which I saw washed off clean and a bit of pencil put between. I could hear the writing distinctly. I wrote questions on slips of paper, folded them up closely, and laid them on the slates, which I held in my two hands. The questions were perfectly answered, and three ticks of the pencil indicated that the writing was finished. On opening them they were filled with writing in a plain hand. The first slate was signed "Mother," expressing great pleasure at having such an opportunity to communicate. The next slate, in a different style, gave a medical prescription, some good advice, and closed with this original verse:

> "Millions and millions of ages shall roll,
> Progression ever the theme of your soul;
> By beauty and grandeur your soul shall be led.
> And worlds without number your spirit shall tread."
> —*Swedenborg.*

I wish to say that in 1867 I spent six months in lecturing on spiritualism through Sonoma, Napa, Santa Cruz, and Sacramento counties, which was a labor of love but not of profit. I have seen materializations and dematerializations once; but do not wish to particularize, as I did not have an opportunity to repeat the sitting so as to study it maturely.

POEMS.

ELECTION RHYMES.

To Doctor Glenn,
I said amen—
And took it back,
But still did lack—
The votes to go
    To Sacramento.

Glenn and I two horses rode,
Along the dry and dusty road,
But we alike were badly thrown,
Before the office found its own.

We dabbled in the filthy pool,
And soiled our garments like a fool,
And yet we were a wretched tool --
    To help the R's to Sacramento.

And now Macvay
Has gained the day—
He will also have his say;
And railroads too will still bear sway,
And Chinamen will learn to pray—
And stock sharps have another day—
And we big taxes still must pay.

And Pellet, too, has lost the race,
Although upon the winning pace—
And up Salt river he must sail,
And like poor Rachel he must wail.

And now the voting all is over,
We'll take a sail up the Salt river,
And farmer White will there appear—
And farmer Gardner in the rear.

Had bilks and chivs joined Farmer White,
The outcome would have been all right—
They would have saved the Golden State,
And next year reached the White House gate.

But now that splendid chance is o'er—
They ne'er will reach the White House more,
Because they put up Doctor Glenn,
And I, alas, did say amen.
—*November, 1878.*

THE MAIDS OF ST. HELENA.

To call one maid divinely fair
When hundreds more are blooming there,
With grace and beauty, rich and rare:
It may be true, but scarce is fair.

True, St. Helena's massive mountain,
And Calistoga's steaming fountain,
O'erlook a valley none surpasses
For stalwart men, and bonny lasses,
For flowers, and vines, and lovely grasses.

On the left is Howell Mountain,
From whose breast springs Conn creek fountain
And wild cascades can there be found,
With rainbows painted on the ground.

On the right Mt. Henry stands,
Whose twin peaks overlook fair lands,
And all the serrate ridge along,
Would claim a mention in a song.

The vineyards on the rounded hill
Instinct with lovely beauty; still
The vineyards on the level plain,
And waving fields of golden grain,

Should surely take a poet's eye,
And not be passed so coldly by.
So over-praise is hardly fair,
When hosts of girls are blooming there.
—*June 1, 1880.*

LINES.

Addressed to Judge and Mrs. W. A. Haskin, at their Golden Wedding.

By John Allyn.

When this old century was young,
Cupid his arrows widely flung,
Until at length his honeyed darts,
Reached their aim and pierced your hearts.

Fifty eventful years have come,
Since your young hearts found a home;
Fifty pregnant years have fled,
Since at the altar you were wed.

Full fifty years of wedded bliss,
Are rare in such an age as this;
When courts are facile—laws are loose,
And often slips the marriage noose.

We greet you here with song and story;
Although your heads are slightly hoary,
Your love is bright and unabated,
As when your young hearts first were mated.

With this world's goods not over-blest,
Like Greeley's young man, you went west:
The placers of our Golden State,
Allured you to your happy fate.

Six months you toiled through dust and rain,
This promised paradise to gain:
Unlike some Western men, I reckon,
You saved your scalps, but not your bacon.

And as the wild Sierras crossed,
And fragrant pines their branches tossed,
The impulse of the vernal wood
Gave you health and moral good.

'Twas thus in eighteen forty-nine,
In woman's glory, manhood's prime;
Our sunny skies and fruitful soil,
Rewarded all your weary toil.

And when you viewed fair Napa's plain,
You wisely said, "We'll here remain;"
Go 'round the world—'tis surely true—
You will not find a fairer view,
Nay, if you search the realms of space,
You'll scarcely find a better place.

One daughter fair,
Of beauty rare,
Among the rest,
Your home has blest.

Seven sons still live to call you blest,
And you have faith that all the rest
Live in a world of greater bliss
Than the most happy can in this.

Your grandchildren who still survive,
Count up at least full thirty-five:
And if your children live and thrive,
They'll swarm like bees in summer hive.

When earthly joys can charm no more,
And Charon kindly rows you o'er,
Your faith is firm that on that shore
You'll there be mated evermore:

That as you join the angel throng,
And countless ages roll along,
Your love will glow still unabated,
As when your youthful hearts were mated.

—*November, 1879*

The effort was a happy one, and its good hits were heartily enjoyed and applauded by the audience, and the Doctor was further rewarded by a bouquet from a fair admirer.—*St. Helena Star*.

ÆTNA SPRINGS (California).

The jagged peaks and rounded mounts
Look out on Ætna's healing founts;
In every little dell around,
Lovely evergreens abound.

Ozone is brought by every breeze
That comes from pine and healing trees,
And every rising sun we see
With silver sheens the lone pine tree.

Under the white oak's spreading boughs
We watch the turn of the polished plows,
While trees upon the sloping hill
The finest sense of beauty thrill.

The moonshine nights and lively jokes
Makes lovers young of wedded folks:
Music floats on the balmy air,
Inspiring each eager, waiting pair
To serve the goddess Terpsichore,
'Till ten o'clock—and sometimes more.

The lowing kine come home at night,
To fill the buckets foaming white;
The ranch gives grapes, so fresh and sweet,
And other fruits to cook and eat,
The lame can walk, the blind can see,
The old are filled with joy and glee.

—*October, 1880.*

THE AMERICAN FLAG.

Lines read by Dr. Allyn at the political meeting, November, 1880.

That flag now floats a nation o'er,
And there 'twill float for evermore;
Surviving foeman's shouts and jeers—
It waved above the loyal cheers.

Let the nation speak in thunder tones,
Echoing from plains to mountain cones—
He who fights against that flag, or trails it in the dust,
Never shall an office hold, or any post of trust.

Full fifty millions free and brave
Live where this splendid banner waves,
And boys and girls are now alive
Who'll see a hundred million thrive.

Let Europe's teeming thousands come
To find with us a happy home,
The ægis of its ample folds
Protects the land and all it holds.

The flag that led the loyal hosts
Now floats in triumph through our coasts;
'Twill save the people brave and pure,
While stars shall shine or sun endure.

The flag that braved a hundred years,
Through battle spark, through rebel cheers,
Shall hold the Union most secure
While moon shall last or sun endure.

POEM.

On the Tenth Anniversary of Dr. and Mrs. G. B. Crane's Wedding

By Dr. John Allyn.

Two Pioneers of great ambition
Sought ample fields for hope's fruition—
You climbed the rugged hill of life
With other husband, other wife—
Both were lured by science and art;
Both took the good Samaritan's part.

The Doctor plied the healing art,
With equal skill and kindly heart;
Not given to work for paltry pelf,
He failed somewhat to "heel" himself.

But when you reached life's summit's crest,
You found you were not wholly blest.

Cheerless—and lonely—the prospect seemed
And life with petty troubles teemed.

Love opened up a splendid vision
And showed you boundless fields elysian—
Love adds a charm to nature's beauty,
And lightens all the paths of duty.

Thus on life's summit there you stand,
With heart to heart and hand to hand;
And being joined with silken tether
Descend the shady slope together.

Society and hosts of friends
And angels shout their glad amens:
True hospitality abounds,
Plenty and peace your home has crowned.

In the sweetest vale of all the earth
The bride was cheered by a blazing hearth,
Plenty of books whose ample pages
Conserved the lore of all the ages.

As if by Madam's magic spell,
This house was raised so nice and well;
But still the hearth and books are found;
Like Banquo's ghost—they will not down.

Science now moves with rapid stride
And ancient landmarks seem to slide—
Better this decade passed away
Than stupid æons of Cathay.

He'd work'd for temperance all his life,
Nor still gave up the noble strife;
If Christ made wine at Cana's feast,
He'd try the "rabbit patch" at least.
If we only had pure wine enough,
It would save from floods of viler stuff.

The once forbidding gravel land
Has smiled beneath your skillful hand;
With wealth your efforts have been crowned,
And generous charities abound.

And now, dear friends, this wedding eve,
Love's tribute here your neighbors leave.
May heaven your blessings still increase,
And guide you to the realms of peace.

DECORATION DAY, 1882.

For the St. Helena celebration. By Dr. John Allyn.

Where rest the dead heroes, once valiant and brave,
The flag of our Union forever shall wave
Over each of our soldiers' well-honored grave.

On this our nation's holiday,
Let patriotic zeal bear sway;
And far as smiling peace is found,
Let pure fraternal love abound.

Rest, soldier, in your hallowed grave—
  Your country's warfare now is o'er;
No cannon's roar will face the brave—
  The drum's roll-beat will call no more.

No bugle's blast will wake from sleep
  And dreams of home or child and wife,
Again to painful vigils keep,
  Or enter into deadly strife.

No dying groans will pierce the air,
　Or wounded comrade writhe in pain;
Where curses mingle with the prayer
　Of him who ne'er will pray again.

Your souls, we trust, will hover round
　And smile serene from viewless air;
As choicest flowers strew the ground,
　Whose fragrance is your country's prayer.

All honor to our soldiers' name—
Naught shall disturb their well-earned fame;
They fought for you, they fought for me,
And countless millions yet to be.

The pomp of war did not allure them—
The press-gangs rough did not procure them:
Their country called, and they obeyed,
And simple duty they essayed.

Some left their aged parents' side;
Some left a blooming, weeping bride;
Some served three years, to then return,
And some were laid beneath the urn.

Go search through history's blood-stained page,
Through every land, through every age—
No warring host that faced each other,
Where brother often fought with brother—
So strove where mind and concience blended,
Until the fearful contest ended.

Grim-visaged War then smoothed his front,
And smiling peace resumed her wont;
And as the loyal work was ended
Each hero's way was wended—
Took up the tangled thread of life,
And strove to comfort child and wife.

The circumstance of glorious war
Had lost its charm; they did abhor
The tedious, fratricidal strife—
Once more adoring civic life.

" 'Othello's occupation 's gone,'
Now this great land is joined in one,"
Was heard throughout this matchless nation,
Without its tragic intonation.

It makes no difference with the brave,
Whether alive or in the grave;
One character pervades them all,
High or low, great or small.

Their memory will never perish—
Their fame a grateful land will cherish
Far as the eagle's pinions spread
Is homage to the nation's dead.

Their spirits haunt the hazy mountains,
And glide about the sparkling fountains;
The smallest rill, the mightiest river,
Flows mingling with their wraiths forever!

And praise the Blue full high you may—
We pass no sentence on the Grey;
Leave them with conscience and with God,
As all are left beneath the sod.

Let all dead issues of the past
No longer live, no longer last;
Live - in the living present live--
To future hopes your efforts give.

Let all unkindness and all hate
Lie buried deep as hopeless fate;
No resurrection give it life,
To ripen in fraternal strife.

Prosperity shall smile forever
O'er hill and lake, o'er plain and river;
Science, high art and education
Shall lift and bless each occupation.

The water dancing from the hills
Shall serve unnumbered cotton mills;
The Mississippi safe shall flow
Between strong dykes from Cairo.

The yellow fever's dreaded scourge
Shall disappear within our verge;
Malarious districts shall be sweet,
And produce amply bread and meat.

Our grand Sierra's snowy crest
Shall overlook a land most blest;
The water from a thousand rills—
From purling streams along the hills—
Shall fertilize the terraced ground,
Where fruit and wheat and vines abound.

Then the Angel of Peace shall utter from far,
Our triumphs, O man, are far better than war!
Save but the result that the slaves were made free,
And the Union preserved for their grand jubilee.

Let patriotic zeal bear sway
On this our Decoration day;
And far as lovely peace is found,
Let pure, fraternal love abound.

IN MEMORIAM. — JAMES L. RIDGELY, 1881.

Read at his funeral celebration by St. Helena Lodge I. O. O. F.

His useful life was quite complete,
With works of love it was replete;
We mourn not that he's gone before,
The loss is ours, his gain is more.

The sympathetic tear will fall
For family, friends, and brothers all.
His spirit leaves the worn-out clay
To seek the realms of endless day.

The first decade our order knew,
Our brother was most firm and true.
Through struggles of each late decade
His laurels bright will never fade.

Our history he's written well;
To latest ages it will tell—
How from the germ of early years
It triumphed o'er its foes and fears.

Ambitious schemes were laid aside;
His faithful work will long abide.
Cities unbuilt will love him well,
And countless hosts his goodness tell.

Odd Fellows will forever cherish
His memory; 'twill never perish.
In distant isles his works abound;
In foreign climes they're also found.

California's sunny plain,
And her piles of golden grain,
From her vineyards, bright and green;
From the Sierra's silvery sheen;

From jagged peaks and rounded hills,
From giant trees and murmuring rills;
From silver mines with golden grains,
From Nevada's sage-brush plains;

From the mountains and the moorland,
From rich prairies and from woodland;
From great cities, commerce-laden,
Come heart tribute, all unbidden.

His fame will rise from sparkling fountains,
And echo from the lofty mountains;
Great lakes will catch the onward strain,
And waft it o'er the ocean's main.

Our Order spreads from State to State,
And has become both strong and great;
Our banner floats in foreign climes,
And will go down to latest times.

The news was spread from shore to shore;
Our brother's earthly toils were o'er.
The sad word all our brothers reaches,
Will ponder well the lesson teaches.

Ridgely has joined the lodge above,
Of fadeless beauty, purest love,
To sing of friendship, love and truth,
With joyful life and fadeless youth.

His earthly work at length is done;
His second life is now begun;
On that bright shore he will progress;
Sages and saints his spirit bless.

Good works on earth will be his joy;
No earthly cares will there annoy;
Distress relieved and orphans blessed,
Will soothe his soul's serenest rest.

REPUBLICAN CAMPAIGN SONG, 1882.

By John Allyn.

Republicans now have a man
Triumphantly to lead the van,
　　While we march on to victory.

The Democrats must now be led
By an official figure-head,
　　As we march on to victory.

The workman's "rest and recreation"
Will then be safe from desecration,
　　When we march on to victory.

No greedy soulless corporation
Can then prevent the recreation,
   Of toiling millions yet to be.

The railroad power now dread the hour
When Morris Estee comes to power,
   To tone down the freights and fares.

No more will they discriminate
Against the struggling of our State,
   When we've marched on to victory.

M. Estee is the coming man,
And foes can beat him if they can,
   While we march on to victory.

Stoneman will surely fail again,
As he did in days of yore, when—
   Sherman marched unto the sea.

I beg that you will all remember
The seventh day of next November,
   For the figure-head
   Will then be dead,
   And Estee be our governor.

WOOLEN WEDDING OF MR. AND MRS. H. E. ALDEN.

By Dr. J. Allyn.

In the roaring loom of time
Some wool is coarse, and some is fine,
And in fabrics made or boughten
The wool is often mixed with cotton.

This symbols forth our mortal life,
Where purest love is marred by strife;
But who'd abide life's hard conditions
If sweetened not by love's fruitions?

For ten long years in town and grove
You reveled in unwedded love—
A lengthy courtship, it would seem,
But quickly passed in love's young dream—
Then found a far more grand ideal
In wedded life amid the real.

The bride was raised with Quaker people,
Who like the church, but not the steeple—
Both plain of dress, and plain of speech,
They very seldom overreach.

But Quaker drab could not control
The tastes of an æsthetic soul;
The highest art of modern dress
That taste alone could well express.

Two children blessed your wedded love;
Alice is here—and one above.
Say not that you have 'loved and lost,'
For when the border you have crossed,
You'll see her bloom with angels bright,
In boundless love and purest white.

From farthest East to utmost West
You sought prosperity and rest.
Prosperity has blessed your store,
And given promise of much more.

Accept our kind congratulations;
We wish auspicious constellations.
These lines express no lofty parts,
But simple tribute of our hearts.

SONG OF HOPE.

By John Allyn.

The jagged peaks and rounded mounts
Look out on Ætna's healing founts,
And every little dell around
With lovely evergreens abound—
And all the smooth, bald ridge along,
Deserves a mention in our song.

The red deer range upon the hill,
And tufted quail, at their sweet will;
And as the wooded mount we cross,
And giant trees their branches toss,
The impulse of the vernal wood
Will give us health and moral good.

Upon the smoothly polished floor
We serve the goddess Terpischore
'Till ten o'clock, and sometimes more;
And every morning sun we see
With silver sheens the lone pine tree.

On Sunday, if we're so inclined,
We seek some loftier good to find—
Inquire our being's end and aim,
And whence this breathing, vital frame.

Why so much sin and suffering here ;
Why life is oft so dull and drear ;
Our anchor, Hope, so often lifted,
As o'er life's stormy seas we're drifted ?

When fleeting breath we cannot keep,
Shall we repose in dreamless sleep,
Or shall we find a fairer shore,
Where sin and suffering are no more ?

Or will a few be highly blest
To view the torture of the rest ?
Can sympathy become quite dead,
And think of this without a dread ?

Though solve these problems as we may,
They vanish with the working day ;
The path of duty still is clear,
And love remains to bless and cheer.

Now lift our souls to orbs of light,
Which sparkle in the dome of night ;
Though space is boundless, still 'twill seem
That law and order reign supreme.
Shall moral chaos curse us here,
And splendid order reign up there ?

The household nursery is a place
Almost devoid of gentle grace ;
The stronger boys will tyrants play,
And gentler sisters must obey ;
The place a very bedlam seems,
Disturbing grandpa's happy dreams.
While fun and frolic rule the hour
There's constant growth to manly power :
Muscle and nerve now have their day
Where moral truth may yet bear sway.

If earth is but the vestibule
Of great Nature's training-school,
Where spirit works through brain and muscle,
Gaining strength with every tussle—
If, passing from this primal school,
We find enjoyment there the rule—

That justice, truth, and love prevail,
And wrong and hate cannot assail :

The "raison d'étre" may appear
To us poor sinners lingering here.
The chain of being is complete
From microscopic wriggler here
To seraph in the upper sphere.

The soul that leaves the worn-out clay
To seek the realms of fairer day,
Will scarce be left without a guide
To aid it through the ethereal tide.
But wheresoe'er a home they find,
They'll surely leave the road behind.
Having grasped his new-found treasure,
And sated with supernal pleasure,
Some sympathy might still be found
For those who walk this solid ground
The place which gave him primal birth
The little globe yclept the earth,
Still might claim some small attention,
And, perchance, some intervention.

But how to reach them—there's the rub.
For, from circumference to the hub,
Men seek their profit or their pleasure
In earnest work—or earnest leisure.

Men send their thoughts unfelt, unseen,
Through oceans' depths, o'er mountains sheen.
If zinc and copper batteries serve,
Why not more perfect brain and nerve
Convey bright thoughts from higher sphere,
To light our groping darkness here?

Some, alas, with truth will say,
We've sought this thing for many a day,
And found that fraud blocked up the way;
We paid our dollar, saw the sight,
And then passed on in doubtful light.

So silver mines were worked by fraud,
And stocks spread ruin all abroad;
But silver mines still yield their treasure
To purchase bread and pay for pleasure;
So grains of truth may yet be found
'Mid heaps of chaff and hollow sound;
The honest seeker sure may find
A healing balm for troubled mind.

—July 15, 1882.

DEMOCRATIC DIRGE.

Had English ponied up the tin,
'Tis sad to think what might have been ;
We might have saved the Hoosier State,
And thus escaped our wretched fate.

Had we got up a glorious boom,
It would have fixed poor Garfield's doom.
The first campaign, way down in Maine,
Proved to us a dreadful bane.

We caught in Weaver's warp and woof,
When we should have stood aloof ;
Money we wanted; all the same,
Hard or soft, it was our game.

The tariff was a local thing.
If voters to us it would bring.
We threw an awful sight of mud,
But to the cause it did no good.

Barnum sold us to the deil,
And no compunction seemed to feel.
Our souls he gripped as in a vice,
And then withheld the pleasant price.

We only gained the golden State,
Just to seal poor Terry's fate ;
And now, alas, the White House door
We ne'er shall enter any more :
   Nevermore, nevermore.

—*November, 1880.*

The "gem" of the evening was the following original poem read by Dr. Allyn in his usual clear and forcible style. At the unanimous request of the club the Doctor has permitted us to publish the same, which we here insert.— *St. Helena Star.*

THANKSGIVING HYMN.

Read at St. Helena Reading Club, November, 1882.

Thou Power Supreme of all the ages,
  That guides and rules the flight of time,
Dimly perceived by seers and sages
  Deign to inspire this humble rhyme.

The orbs that roll through boundless space
 And twinkle in the dome of night,
May teach our souls some gentle grace
 And fill our hearts with thanks and light.

Some worlds abound with lurid fire,
 No sentient thing can breathe or live;
Some sputter still with seething mire
 But lowest forms of life can give.

We thank the Power of Life Supreme,
 Our lot is cast in latest ages,
Though all the past seems but a dream
 As back we turn great Nature's pages.

Species in countless hosts abound
 Who greatly fear--or truly love us,
We're lord of all beneath--around,
 And only angels still above us.

We're thankful that our lot is cast
 Where Freedom's soil is unpolluted,
No despot's hand the State has grasped
 And manhood's joys are undiluted.

We bless Thee that our lot is cast
 To reap the noblest fruits of Time,
If we but learn from all the past
 To make humanity sublime.

We're grateful that within our border
 Gentle peace now smiles serene.
And everywhere are law and order,
 And brightest hopes spring fresh and green.

No pestilential deadly scourge
 Fills our land with woe and mourning;
No unruled passions seethe and surge,
 The people's hearts to strife returning.

With rapturous joy our hearts o'erflow
 That worship now is free as air,
No persecution's demon blow
 Can blight the budding flowers of prayer.

Our grateful hearts with thanks abound
 That through our glorious, happy land,
Good education now is found
 To foster truth with liberal hand.

We bless the Power of Life Sublime
That field and forest, stream and glen,
Abound with choicest fruits of time
To satisfy the needs of men.

And on this Pilgrims' festal day
Whether the sky be bright or murky,
Whatever else we do or say,
We're truly thankful for the turkey.

ANNIVERSARY CELEBRATION OF ST. HELENA LODGE, I. O. O. F.

By JOHN ALLYN.

On this anniversary meeting
Of Odd Fellows' joyful greeting,
From aged sire to fiery youth
We sing of "Friendship, Love, and Truth."

Imagination's soaring wing,
Or fancy's high esthetic taste,
Might tempt sublimer themes to sing,
Still all might prove a dreary waste.

While others seek the bauble fame,
And wear their lives out for a name,
Our souls should strive to rise above
And live for Friendship, Truth, and Love.

We place no chains on human thought,
For mind is never to be bought;
Believe and vote just as you will—
Cherish fraternal friendship still.

We've constantly increased our store;
We've scattered much—but gathered more;
All in prosperous days must give,
That sweetest charity may live.

When husbands pass the mortal border,
Widows have cause to bless our Order;
Our orphans we must educate—
Visit the sick—their pains abate,
Relieve distress wherever found,
Our dead we place beneath the ground.

This Lodge has kept these maxims well
   As all our history will tell
Prosperity has smiled serene,
   And brightest hopes spring fresh and green.

Thirteen years this lodge has flourished;
   Full ninety members it has nourished
In pleasant bonds of love fraternal,
   And let us hope they'll prove eternal.

—January 20, 1883.

HALF A CENTURY AGO.

(Supplement to the Barkhamsted Reminiscences, No. Twenty-Two.)

By JOHN ALLYN.

Sweet strawberries grew on the meadow sandy,
And for roving boys they were very handy,
And under the grass along the hill,
A hungry lad could find his fill.
I've been where writers ever boast,
Along the famed Pacific coast,
That berries ripen through the year—
Although the hills are brown and sere,
Though large, luscious, and red—but still
They were sweeter far on my native hill.

Along the grand Pacific slope
Where salmon to river-fountains grope—
Where the darkly speckled native trout
Came spying in, and darting out—
But the sweetest trout that ever I took
With small scoop-net, or barbed hook,
Were caught in the pools of Beaver brook.

The little brown school-house on the green
Will never lose its charming sheen,
And school-mates! ah! most have gone before,
I trust to find a brighter shore.
And my teachers? I learn that some still live,
And may they enjoy what God can give.

Not far away is a water-worn ledge,
Nature's record of the great Ice Age—
I filled my pockets with arrow-heads,
Rifled from the makers' native bed,
That tell of a race that have long since fled.

—1883.

SONS OF BARKHAMSTED.

From Litchfield county has gone forth,
The greatest preacher of the earth ;
For fiction of the moral cast,
H. B. Stowe's was ne'er surpassed.

Barkhamsted's sons are scattered wide,
From the Hudson's swelling tide,
To where the surging breakers roar
Along the grand Pacific shore.

In New York's busy marts of trade
Some solid fortunes have been made,
Though tricks of trade are plenty there;
Some were made upon the Squire.

The broad Ohio's teeming soil
Was settled by our sons of toil;
In Chicago's moral city
Dwell our people, wise and witty.

And richer prairies farther west
Have been highly tilled and blessed,
By native sons of vale and hill
Who God's great primal law fulfill.

They've grasped the elements of wealth,
And had an eye to schools and health—
The lumber pines of Minnesota,
The unrivaled wheat fields of Dakota.

The cotton on the Mexique main,
The cattle on the Texas plain—
The silver mines with golden sands,
And California's matchless lands.

Of learned men a goodly share
Have had their birth and training there:
Doctors, lawyers, judges, preachers,
From Richardson to Amos Beecher.

One genius high, of talents rare,
With common men beyond compare,
Who sought to unfold a new religion—
To open clear to mortal vision
From sordid earth to highest heaven :
The prophet Joel honor won
Excepting in his native town.

Of all the men of talent rare
Whose memory will linger there,
One rhyming Poet stands alone,
Though long since passed to his long home.

TO MISS MARY L. HART.

This we say of Barkhamsted town,
 It has no great, or wide renown
A land of meadows, rocks and hills
 Of timber trees, and water mills.

But these rugged, sterile mountains,
 Burling rills, and sparkling fountains,
Have nourished men of sterling worth,
 And women bright, the salt of earth.

Its history was fading fast,
 And swift receding to the past—
Oblivion's gulf would soon receive
 All that we know, or e'en believe.

Our heroine then gave her Hart
 To act the true historian's part—
This history in every part
 Will honor both her head and heart.

The dark clouds of a troubled day
 Her cheerful spirits drive away;
She in her constant happy mood
 Forgets herself for others' good.

Her dark and glossy curling hair
 Denotes the genius sleeping there;
Her darkly bright and sparkling eyes
 And light complexion do likewise.

Dear friend, continue on your work.
 You seldom falter, never shirk.
Your memory we all hold dear.
 Though silent long, you need not fear.

The monument you now uprear
 To many thousands will appear,
When zinc and marble fade and rust—
 Earth to earth and dust to dust.

THE SPARKLING RAIN.

By John Allyn.

The parched fields cry rain, more rain.
When shall we feel its patter again?
'Tis here, 'tis here, the glorious rain,
The thirsty fields are moist again.

The rain, the rain, the sparkling rain,
We hail with joy its patter again.
By it the banker counts his gain,
By it the farmer grows his grain.

The cattle roaming on the hill,
Now can crop a generous fill
Of luscious grass bedecked with flowers,
And grapes will hang from maidens' bowers.

The ships of ocean shall have their freight
Of wheat that is plump and full in weight.
For the rain, the rain, has come again,
And merchants now can count their gain.

The rain, the rain, the sparkling rain,
We hail with joy its patter again.
It brings us wealth, it brings us life,
With choicest blessings it is rife.

By it we see the rainbow of hope,
By it the doors of plenty we ope.
The rain, the rain, the welcome rain,
We are thankful to hear its patter again.

Soon, warm and fine, the sun will shine,
To ripen and sweeten our ruby wine.
'Tis good for the sick, 'tis good for us all,
If only we heed kind nature's call.

March, 1884.

CAMPAIGN LINES.

Read at St. Helena, October, 1884.

The Democratic cause is weak,
Their standard-bearer still more weak,
The inert mass they try to leaven
By principles that count up seven--

Five small loaves and two small fishes,
Their utmost hopes—their ardent wishes.
The toiling voters may compete
With heavy laden merchant fleet,
Freighted with Europe's and Asia's toil,
Our manufactories to despoil.

The dudes are few and growing scarce,
Ashamed of such a wretched farce;
Too pure at first to vote for Blaine,
They sickened quite at Cleveland's fame.

The dudes of York, the dudes of Yale,
Soon will morn, and weep, and wail,
To see their free-trade notions fail.

The Irish vote will be divided
Because they have not been provided
Many will vote for James G. Blaine
For taking the lion by the mane.
They like to hear him rave and roar,
Now they're far from Albion's shore.

Butler will help our cause along
By taking off the cranky throng.

Republicans are crowned with glory,
Long will they live in song and story.
And for a grand, inspiring slogan
We've statesman Blaine and soldier Logan.
Our postal service is far better;
From two-bits—to two cents a letter.
We've built three roads from shore to shore,
And capital will build us more.
In finance—Utopia's beau-ideal,
Our statesmanship has made the real—
Greenbacks and bonds, silver and gold,
All are at par where goods are sold.
We give to settlers an ample farm
To save from want and add home's charm.
We've saved united this great nation.—
Raised every slave to freeman's station.
Our cause is strong—our leaders stronger—
And we'll hold the fort a little longer.

TO DR. AND MRS. G. B. CRANE.

Read at Mrs. Crane's Rose Party, November 16, 1883. By DR. JOHN ALLYN.

Roses bloom in great variety,
   But never cause the least satiety;
The last rose of summer is ever in mind,
   But roses of winter to us are more kind.

The rose by itself for beauty ne'er lacks,
   But your taste prefers it trimmed with smilax;
We speak not of that which they call a flower,
   Though seen in your sweet home bower.

The roses of war, destruction and hate,
   Are names that cover a terrible fate;
The rose we love is a rose of Peace,
   Which sweetly will bloom when all wars cease.

Roses of art may play a fine part
   In finishing milliner's goods,
Though always in bloom, they shed no perfume,
   And so are but partially good.

Wild roses bloom by murmuring streams
   Where the sun shines down in broken beams;
Their petals are sparse, and rough and rude
   Where no fair helping hands intrude.

Of cultured roses there's endless variety;
   To name and describe with strict propriety,
Would take more paper and ink and time
   Than can well be spared to this brief rhyme.

The rose that all are praising
   Is our generous, gentle hostess,
This may appear amazing
   But is said without a boast.

FOR THE GOLDEN WEDDING OF MR. AND MRS. ARETAS HARDY.

BY JOHN ALLYN.

When this old century was new,
   Bright Cupid's arrows wildly flew,
Until at length his hurried darts
   Reached their aim—and pierced your hearts.

In Maine's primeval forest mountains,
  And from her pure and sparkling fountains,
Two gentle purling streams flowed on
  Until they both were joined in one.

Like the symbolic living river,
  They will thus flow on forever.
All this is but a symbol chosen
  Of these two hearts thus joined by heaven.

In Industry* the bride was reared,
  And industry she's always shared;
She always was both hale and hearty,
  But marriage made her still more Hardy.

You've lived at home always together
  In sunshine bright, and stormy weather;
You were so loving and true-hearted,
  You've only been quite briefly parted.

Your happy home one son has blessed,
  Three lovely daughters you've caressed.
Two are still on the hither shore,
  And one—not dead, but gone before.

Of grandchildren you've half a score,
  And may expect unnumbered more;
They're all a comfort to your age,
  Whose names would grace this rhythmic page.

Fifty full years of wedded bliss
  Are rare in such an age as this,
When courts are facile, laws are loose,
  And often slip the marriage noose.

Three score years you've spent in Maine,
  The native place of statesman Blaine;
A rugged clime of mount and glen,
  Prolific most of noted men.

In California's genial clime
  Full sixteen years you passed like rhyme;
In Napa's vale you dwelt awhile,
  And left too soon for city's wile.

Old age is coming on apace,
  And soon you'll close your earthly race.
The mystery of coming years
  May bring you joy unmixed with tears.

---

* Industry is the name of the town where the bride was born.

And now, good friends, this wedding eve
   With you love's offerings here we leave;
May choicest blessings still increase,
   And smooth your path to blessed peace.

TWO ASPECTS OF NATURE.

Written for the Literary Club by JOHN ALLYN.

I.

In this world of evolution,
With now and then a revolution,
Success is never quite complete,
And failure is with hope replete.

Could we scan the inmost being,
And our envious self-love freeing,
We should find the great and good
Were only partly understood.

With outward signs of wealth and state,
And honors heaped upon the great,
Lurk grov'ling passions, doubt and gloom,
Awaking fears of coming doom.

Who gathers riches, adds to care,
And often weaves his soul a snare;
His happiness is often seeming,
His fears and trouble often teeming.

II.

Of those who fall out by the ways,
And scarcely live out half their days,
We might find very much to praise,
Most worthy of a poet's lays.

Could we but scan the true beginning
Of the souls most deeply sinning,
We'd see them hounded to their fate,
And aided not by Church or State.

The germs of all that's good and wise,
Would pulsate there before our eyes;
But, overborne by passion's power,
Outwrought before the natal hour.

This world is but the vestibule
Of great Nature's training school:
Harmonious development
Will sure result when passion's spent.

In that bright world of joy and glory,
But little known to song and story;
All will harmonious growth attain,
And thus through endless time remain.

Much that now is dark and dreary,
There will be both light and cheery;
The grandeur of the glorious whole
Will thrill with pleasure every soul.

The economy of evolution
Will light up clearly retribution,
As day and night must come and go,
As ocean's tides must ebb and flow.

So good and evil interblend,
But high achievement is the end,
And the merest recreation
Works out the highest exaltation.

'Tis true that some are crushed and bruised,
And always seem to be abused;
Justice is but a partial force,
While harmony will crown the course,

A Man's Thoughts on the Woman Question.

READ BEFORE THE ST. HELENA WOMAN-SUFFRAGE ASSOCIATION BY
DR. JOHN ALLYN.

As prefatory to a direct consideration of the subject, I wish distinctly to repudiate what is sometimes expressed or implied, that there is an antagonism between the rights and interests of men and women. So long as every man *must* have a mother, *should* be a husband, and *may* be the father of daughters, so long, whatever tends to enlarge the sphere of woman, to elevate her, morally, intellectually, and physically, is directly calculated to benefit man and improve society.

This subject is engaging a large share of the attention of intelligent, earnest, thinking people, both in this country and the older, more fossilized civilizations of Europe. For years there has been a manifest tendency to enlarge woman's sphere, as it is called, in the walks of industry, literature, science, and art. With scarcely an exception, this movement is regarded by intelligent persons as a healthy progress and a beneficent prophecy of the future.

I regard woman suffrage as but a branch, an important one, it is true, of this entire movement. Power is a necessary element in human conditions, and political governments wield an immense power over the destinies of the people. Hitherto, that power has come far short of achieving the highest possible good; nor do I for a moment suppose that the addition of a new element, which I would term the female element, in politics and legislation would at once achieve all possible good or avoid all evil incident to human governments. We are apt to regard institutions and usages as fixed, whereas the thinker perceives that all things are but growths more or less gradual. The globe we inhabit is the growth of time; much of the solid rock is formed by gradual accretions from aqueous sedimentary deposits or the labors of minute animals; the soil is formed by the slow disintegration of more solid rocks and mixtures of vegetable mold accumulated from year to year through the ages. Governments and religions are also growths of time, and both are far from having reached a condition which scientists term one of stable equilibrium. Sad indeed would it be were nothing further to be achieved even in our own favored land where government has done more for the people than in any other age or country of our globe. Yes; inspiration and intuition have alike discerned a good time coming, from the prophets of Israel to the seers of America, when nations should not destroy each other in warfare or politicians pervert or waste the substance of the people.

From our standpoint, recognizing the natural right of woman to achieve all in the fields of industry or intellect that her natural powers enable her to; there are laws, and the greater power behind the laws — public sentiment — which are wrong and need removing or reforming. But I repudiate the idea sometimes thoughtlessly advanced, that man has acted in bad faith towards woman and consciously framed laws to oppress or enslave her. As a rule, the laws were made from a noble purpose to subserve alike the interests of man and woman. As an example, take one of the laws complained of, which requires the estate of a deceased married man to pass into the hands of an administrator. In times past, women have been so unacquainted with business matters that such a law was necessary to protect them from spoliation from designing knaves. It is doubtful whether a sufficient number of women are acquainted with business to render it safe for their interest to change such a law. It is at first requisite that woman should be trained in business sufficient to protect herself, and then the law should be changed to meet the progressed condition of society.

But while we maintain that the laws affecting women more particularly have resulted from honest efforts to meet the necessities of the case and promote the best interests of women, yet they have been made by that portion of humanity who can only look at the subject from a masculine standpoint and through masculine eyes. However much he may desire to do justice, man cannot fully appreciate the feelings and needs of woman; therefore the feminine half of the people should be directly represented in legislatures to secure the highest and best legislation. Were such the case, I feel satisfied that many laws would be improved. As to the objection that there would be more political intrigue and wire-pulling than now, suffice it to say that then, as now, that will rest with the people. If there is sufficient intelligence and moral stamina among the people to demand honesty in their political servants, they will have it; if not, Heaven help them! It is said that women are more ambitious of the honors of office than men. Whatever of truth there is in this results from the plain fact that man's ambition is counterbalanced by the difficulties which beset the pathway of the political aspirant. If a woman is afflicted with an inordinate ambition for place, for power, and for distinction, a little experience in the labors, the struggles, and the disappointments incident to office-seeking would afford an effective antidote.

The idea has prevailed in society that girls have no legitimate career but to become wives and mothers; to this end are they educated and trained; and if they succeed, they become a household ornament or a houshold drudge, according to the circumstances of their husbands; but for those who fail to secure husbands in early life, for any cause, there is no honorable and inviting career open.

In more recent years, a few possessing uncommon energy to outface public sentiment have made their way to respectable positions as preachers, physicians, writers, sculptors, and painters; but to the great majority life becomes a disappointment, a dreary waste; and amidst the sneers of the low-minded, they gravitate to the wretched position of a governess in a brother's or a sister's family, without the wages of a governess.

While this is the result of Protestant sentiments, usages, and education, the Catholic Church has provided within her ample pale an honorable and useful career for this class which, in older countries where there are more females than males, is always large. They can enter the service of the Church and be useful, respected, and happy, in educating and caring for the orphan and ministering to the sick; and in times of war and pestilence, the Sisters of Charity become Angels of Mercy to the maimed, the suffering, and the dying. Protestantism presents but a transitional phase of society, and is inadequate to meet the needs of all classes of society; and there remains, then, but the alternative to go back to Catholicism, or forward to a better condition of society yet to be evolved by the struggles of reformers.

Maternity is, doubtless, the crowning honor of woman; but all are not privileged to participate in the happiness and honor of rearing healthy, intelligent, and moral sons and daughters; and any woman whose constitution is such that a physiologist could perceive that she could not become the mother of such children, does herself a great wrong, and society a still greater wrong, to become a mother; or, further, if a woman prefers to forego maternity and devote her energies to achievements in the fields of industry, reform, benevolence, literature, art, or science, she should be respected in so doing; and such a course might prove more useful to the world than to be the mother of any number of children below the average.

The Catholic Church is a mother to her daughters, and before our Protestant civilization can supply her place, woman must be so educated and trained as to be self-poised, self-reliant, self-supporting, and inspired with other aims in life than to be merely some man's wife and pet. But it is said, " this involves great labors, great responsibilities, and is beset with insurmountable difficulties." True, the difficulties are great, but energy, perseverance, and a definite aim, will accomplish wonders; and we should not forget that faculties and powers, both physical and mental, increase with use, and these become still further augmented by inheritance from mother to daughter.

I am satisfied that men are more ready to grant equal political, educational, and industrial privileges than women are to ask for them with a serious intent to actually improve them. This is indicated by the action of the regents of the California University. On the application of the first young woman to participate in its high privileges, the doors were opened alike to young women and young men.

True, some trades unions have acted on a narrow and selfish principle—like the typographical union—in trying to exclude women; but on the same narrow and selfish principle, many industrial guilds have actually compelled master workmen to exclude the great majority of boys from learning trades, that they might command the work and dictate the rate of wages. These are exceptional cases where blind selfishness got the better of the broader principles of justice, which are of more universal application. It is easy to perceive that the principal opponents of this movement are women; and these may be divided into two classes: First, the wealthy classes—women who have prosperous, kind, indulgent husbands and have formed habits of luxurious ease, and sometimes of wasteful extravagance. These "have all the rights they want;" and with ample means to cultivate social and æsthetic tastes, they do not care to trouble themselves with the sterner labors of understanding political problems, which they will have to do in self-protection if Biddy is allowed to vote. To this class may be added Mrs. General Thus, and the Honorable Mrs. So-and-So, who are delighted to appropriate the honor of their husbands' achievements, without the trouble of making any achievements for themselves. All these are the few who have drawn prizes in the lottery of life and are determined to enjoy their advantages to the full without cultivating a troublesome appreciation of the needs of the many who have failed to draw prizes in the aforesaid lottery. Second, the larger ignorant class, made up of various phases of ignorance. This class is led by political, religious, or social demagogues, aided by that giant impersonal demagogue — public sentiment. This last class is most numerous and most formidable. Fortune is fickle, the votaries of ease and pleasure are weak and inefficient opponents, but ignorance and prejudice are very tenacious; and like the fabled vampire, they prey upon their victims. To remedy this, we must inspire with lofty aims for self-culture and personal achievement. The struggle, discipline, and development incident to obtain the ballot will be a useful preparation for its judicious use.

There is at the present time a frightful amount of matrimonial infelicity in civilized society, to express by a mild term what might be more forcibly expressed by the term "conjugal pandemoniums." There are a great variety of causes for this unfortunate state of social life. Bad men and bad liquors are accountable for much, but it lies in the line of this address to mention a prolific cause of inharmonious households which this movement promises to relieve. It consists in a diversity of aims in life and a diversity of education and training in the candidates for matrimony. The young man who has to make his own way in the world mainly, and who has a purpose to be something more than a cipher, realizes the necessity of accumulating capital; to accomplish this it is necessary to live prudently, and add economy to industry. The young lady, not having been subjected to the wholesome discipline of earning money, has no adequate appreciation of capital as a factor in the affairs of life—is intent on living as her quondam schoolmate, Alice Angelina, lives, who may be in quite different circumstances. Thus while one member of the partnership is intent on accumulating, and the other spending those accumulations in fashionable display which might well be avoided, in part at least, there arises an irrepressible conflict.

The indications then, plainly are, that girls should learn some profession or business as well as boys, by which they can earn an honorable living, in case they never choose to marry, or meet with misfortunes in life, or become orphans or widows. Many professions and branches of industry are now open to women; others will be, as the movement progresses. There are now in the United States seven medical colleges expressly for women, besides many others where they are admitted on an equality with men. True, the grade of scholarship in some of these is not of the highest order, but even the lowest grade will serve to prepare women to become nurses and accoucheurs, and to elevate those professions. Much of journalism and type-setting, not requiring great physical strength, seem fit employments for women.

In the East, where there is an excess of women over men, editors are constantly receiving letters inquiring what industrial occupations are open to women; the demand seems greater than the supply, but we should reflect that our industrial conditions are rapidly changing; mere muscle is not likely to be at the same premium in the future that it has been in the past.

In the last half century much rough work has been done that will not have to be repeated; the vast forests of western New York, Pennsylvania, Ohio, and Indiana have been cleared—the prairies of Illinois, Iowa, and Wisconsin are broken up and reduced to cultivation—the placer mines of the Pacific Slope nearly exhausted, and the crests of the Rocky Mountains and the Sierras scaled and spanned by one of the finest railroads in the world. Add to this that machinery is constantly being brought to do what muscle formerly did, and that we are likely to have an oversupply of laborers from China to do such uncongenial rough labor as remains to be done. The greater portion of the most laborious and exhausting farm labor is now done by machinery. Thus the tendency of our civilization is to diversify industry, and afford to all an opportunity to select an occupation somewhat suitable to tastes and capacities—that all men and women may enjoy the God-given right to earn an independent and honorable livelihood, and, working out their own destiny, make such achievements as their capacity, industry, and perseverance may permit.

Prompted by the generous bounty of the federal government, California has provided the facilities, free alike to young men and young women, to acquire a complete university and professional education, without paying one dollar for tuition fees. The pupil who graduates from the public high school can enter the fifth class of the University—passing through that, can enter the University, and after graduating in that, can study any of the learned professions. To those who wish to prepare for the respectable occupation of a teacher the open doors of the State Normal School invite all alike. To those who wish to pursue any of the natural sciences the University affords ample facilities.

There are now fifteen young women acquiring a medical education in the Medical department of the University of Michigan. How long shall California lag behind the Banner State of educational progress?

—*1872.*

MISCELLANEOUS.

THE PETRIFIED FOREST.

St. Helena, May 5, 1872.

Editor Transcript:—It is understood that a tourist cannot "see" California without visiting three well-heralded wonders of nature. These are Yosemite Valley and Falls, the Big Trees, and the Geysers. But though less known, the Petrified Forest is scarcely less interesting to the geologist, the mineralogist, or the lover of the wonderful in nature. This is situated four miles west of Calistoga hot spring (a small village whose name indicates its character), situated at the head of Napa Valley. It is located on a ridge of the Coast Range Mountains dividing Napa and Sonoma valleys, at an elevation of about two thousand feet above the sea.

On inquiring the way to this remarkable phenomenon of some settlers residing in the neighborhood, I was gratuitously informed that the Petrified Forest was a humbug. Truly there is no accounting for taste. I suppose that some men have lived all their lives within hearing of the roar of Niagara without ever taking the trouble to see it. If public opinion would tolerate such a thing, they might call it a humbug.

As we leave Calistoga, ascending the hill at an easy grade, St. Helena mountain affords some grand and beautiful scenery. At a distance of about five miles it lifts its rugged majestic cone 4,400 feet above the sea-level. Knights Valley, checked with fields of growing crops in dark-green, pea-green, and variegated colors, set in a framework of noble forests and mountain shrubbery in the rich foliage of spring, afforded a charming prospect. On reaching the ground we find its hilly surface of the cretaceous formation abounding in volcanic tufa. The trees lie scattered about over nearly 100 acres, and some at a greater distance. They are from two to ten feet in diameter, often broken quite squarely across, three or four feet in length, almost as if they had been sawed for cord wood, but some of the lengths were broken into fragments, affording an abundance of specimens to be carried away by visitors. These pieces show the grain—sometimes a knot or a curl—as plainly as the fresh-cut wood, while one side will glitter with fine quartz crystal. As a Boston man recently appropriated a generous quantity of these specimens, I presume you can see some in the Boston Museum. A party of geologists from the University of California recently visited this place; their ideas will soon be made public as to the formation of these petrifactions. The largest tree has a trunk of sixty feet, unbroken, lying above ground, the remainder being buried in the hill side. It is rather plain that these petrifactions were redwood, oak and fir, the only trees that abound to any extent in the vicinity at the present time. As redwood logs have been cut in artesian wells in Oakland at a depth of several hundred feet, it is presumed they have flourished here for a length of time not easily determined. These petrifactions are thought by some to be formed by the action of water holding silica in solution. They might have flourished in a basin which had gathered a soil from the surrounding hills, whose outlet was a narrow precipitous gorge that might have been so stopped by an earthquake or volcanic eruption as to flood the basin. We may as well rest with this conjecture until science shall determine the character and cause of the phenomena.

EVOLUTION AND RELIGION.

REPLY TO A SERMON.

A religious teacher who arrays religion against science will impair the force of the moral truths he may utter. Personal religion consists in purity of heart and purpose, and righteousness of life. Efforts to promote these, however humble, will be respected; but efforts to array religion against the eternal verities of science, will not.

Theism does not enter into the problem of evolution at all. Because we, as individuals have sprung from minute beginnings by gradual growth, it does not follow that God is not our Author or Creator. Precisely so as to the origin of animal life, including man, on this planet. If the whole sprung from minute beginnings by a process of gradual growth or evolution, it in no way affects the question of the Power or the Person who was the moving force. The question of evolution among well-informed scientists is regarded as settled as firmly as the law of gravitation or the circulation of the blood in the animal system.

At Harvard, every professor whose department is connected with biology (living or extinct animal forms) is an evolutionist—Asa Gray, Whitney, A. Agassiz, Hagan, Goodale, Shaler, Farlow, Faxon. At the Johns Hopkins University, which aims to be in the van of advancement, evolution is held and taught. In the University of Pennsylvania all the biological Professors are evolutionists—Leidy, Allen, Rother, and Parker. At Yale, Dartmouth, Cornell, Michigan, Brown, Bowdoin, and Princeton Universities the biological Professors are in the same category. Many of these are conservative men and Theists.

The establishment of the law of evolution is by most scientists regarded as the greatest achievement of the century.

Darwin takes a high place as a scientist and benefactor of mankind—what his religious opinions are does not appear from his works. He sailed over oceans and traveled over continents, carefully noting what he observed, and systematized the fruits of his labor without mentioning their relations to God or religion. He was a high-minded, conservative English gentleman, whose love of truth and knowledge predominated over prejudices and preconceived theories.

It is nearly ten years since in a scientific association an English clergyman asked Professor Huxley if he really wished it understood that he had descended from a monkey. Huxley got up in the learned body and calmly said, "If I had any choice in the matter—which clearly I have not—I should prefer to be descended from a monkey, than from a clergyman of the Church of England, who makes no better use of his brains than to oppose science and ridicule its cultivators." This brought down the house and put a quietus to his clerical friend.

SCIENCE AND RELIGION.

CONSISTING OF CRITICISMS AND SUGGESTIONS.

" Prove all things ; hold fast that which is good."

During the present century science has made solid achievements with a rapidity unparalleled in history; this has been looked upon with alarm by some well-wishers of humanity as imperiling morality and religion. Religion has not progressed so fast as science for two reasons. Its postulates are not objects of the senses, and its creeds are supposed to be based on the positive inspiration of a perfect intellect. And although creeds are widely departed from in the religious teachings of the times, and still wider by the popular belief, they for the most part remain unrewritten.

It need scarcely be said that the word "religion" is used in its theoretical or systematic sense, as less liable to objection than the word "theology."

Probably the greatest achievement science has ever made, not excepting the discovery of the law of gravitation, is the recognition of evolution as an established law as universal as the law of gravitation, governing the formation of planetary systems, the genesis and growth of animal and vegetable life, the progress of civilization, government, and society. Evolution is now almost universally recognized by scientists. Ten years ago it was warmly contested, but now probably nineteen twentieths of college professors accept it, and the standing of the other twentieth renders their opinions of no importance. This great achievement, whose fruits have scarcely commenced to ripen, will yet do much for the improvement of human conditions. We are indebted for this great boon to the life-long labors of such men as Herbert Spencer, Darwin, Lyell, Huxley, and Professor O. C. Marsh of Yale college.

Some well-meaning people have been unnecessarily exercised lest this doctrine should undermine morality and religion. It may indicate that the first chapters of Genesis have the imperfections characteristic of most human productions and will have to be reinterpreted. The most able theologians accept this; but the great essential doctrines of religion, the future life, and the existence of an overruling Intelligence, remain unaffected by it. The atheist holds that the universe has been evolved by the action of the ultimate atoms and molecules as acted upon by the law or force of gravitation, chemical affinity, electricity, and all the natural forces, and nothing else.

The intelligent religionist, acknowledging the evolutionary action of all these, holds that the primal force moving all is the will of the Supreme Intelligence. Science can neither affirm nor deny this proposition. A scientist may be an agnostic; he may say, "I do not know that there is a God," but scientifically he cannot deny that there is a governing Intelligence. Admitting the existence of such a being, evolution simply shows the mode by which creation has been effected, and nothing more. The being and character of God must be relegated to theology, as wholly beyond the reach of science, which concerns itself with such facts and phenomena as may be verified by the human senses and human reason.

With the other essential doctrine of religion, to wit, the continuance of human life after the death of the body, it is different. If it exists, it is reasonable to suppose that it admits of scientific verification; and certainly it cannot be scientifically denied except after an exhaustive examination.

We should not be deterred in this examination by the sentiment, held by some, that materialism affords no basis for sound morality. A complete knowledge of the facts in the case, whatever they may prove to be, must afford the best possible grounds for the best possible morality for well-developed intellectual beings. And that morality which is dependent on the terrors of an orthodox hell, or any arbitrary punishment after death, does not extend below the "cutis vera." That man's education, or perhaps I should say development, is very incomplete, who cannot, unblanched, look annihilation squarely in the face. Astronomers tell us that the centrifugal force of the earth is gradually becoming exhausted and that its final destiny is to fall into the sun. Should this occur, it must in a short time mingle with his molten masses or be dissipated in vapor; in which event it becomes a grave question what will become of all individualities which have had a genesis or a habitat on this planet. Other possible astronomical catastrophes may knock the whole solar system into fine dust, like an exploded meteor—and what then?

Plainly, what is required to promote the interests of true religion and sound morality is more light, a better knowledge of the prime elements of the problem with which we have to deal. To get this light, I assume that we should proceed according to the Baconian or scientific method; that is, to first carefully examine the facts or premises in the case. The wrong attitude of the people in this regard has retarded the acquisition of this light; and to more clearly express myself, I shall now proceed to criticise the attitude and conduct of three classes of people, viz., the spiritualists, the religionists, and the scientists.

SPIRITUALISM.

Spiritualism is the logical successor of previous beliefs; hence, sincere themselves, they lay too great stress on mere belief, and as a religious sect are too intolerant of critical investigation. The slate-writing and rapping phenomena are not easily explained, and may indicate the existence of some law or force not recognized by science, but fall short of proving the fact of spirit agency; but when we come to the latest and highest manifestation—the materialization of spirits—we are disappointed. In San Francisco, a professed performance of this kind has been exhibited six nights in a week for the last four years; which is nothing but clumsy, transparent fraud. If it rose to the dignity of a clever feat of legerdemain, there would be some compensation for the dollar charged for admission. In justice, I must say that some spiritualists repudiate these, while others will not only not expose it themselves, but will frown upon any who should essay the task. We read in the organ of the sect of better phenomena of this kind at Terre Haute, Memphis, Boston, New York, and other eastern cities, but the failure of anything of the kind in San Francisco raises fear that distance lends enchantment to the view. Nothing will allay this but a thorough, critical, personal examination under strictly test conditions.

It is a little strange that religionists, while lamenting the growth of materialism and deprecating its influence, should so bitterly oppose spiritualism, the only means of arresting it. In making this sweeping charge I must make some exceptions. It seems plain that, intellectually and philosophically, the great struggle of the age is between religion and materialism; and that the triumph of spiritualism is the only means that can save religion. Some years ago some remarkable phenomena were supposed to have occurred in the Clark residence in Oakland. The accounts published in the daily papers were highly sensational and exaggerated, still they were considered of sufficient importance to be investigated by a committee of learned and intelligent citizens. After due investigation, this committee came to this lame and impotent conclusion: "We do not find evidence that the phenomena were caused by supernatural causes." The public hoped from this committee to have a statement of the facts proved and what were traceable to fraud or trickery. And the committee ought to have known that spiritualists have never claimed a supernatural origin for any of their phenomena; on the contrary, their writers and speakers, from the first raps at Hydeville, N. Y., thirty odd years ago, taught that they were strictly natural; that the realm of nature and law extended into the spiritual world and governed spirits out of the body as much as those still in the flesh. With these remarks I will leave the Church, commending to the kind care of the clergy the large and increasing number of their flocks who are believers in spiritualism and seeking light and comfort at its shrine.

SCIENCE.

It now remains to pay my respects to the scientists; and truth compels me to say they have treated the matter with unmitigated bigotry and intolerance, ignoring the great principles of investigation they have professed since the days of Francis Bacon, and by the aid of which they have made their grand achievements. Professor Huxley, whose great talents, profound metaphysical grasp, great attainments in biological science, and limpid, charming style, render his writings sought and read with avidity wherever the English language is spoken, said: "Even if the spiritual phenomena are true, they do not interest me."

The more is the pity.

In defense, they cannot say they are too frivolous and barren to deserve attention from those who can find a fossil skeleton to study, for this will hardly avail when such eminent scientists as Crooks of London and Wallace, Zollner of Germany have thought them worthy of their best attention and labor. The great physiologist, Dr. Carpenter, has written and published a volume to refute and expose spiritualism; persists from beginning to end in speaking of them as supernatural, thus showing that he has failed to inform himself of the elements of the problem he discusses, or that he designedly misrepresents in order to throw discredit on a matter he fails to meet squarely.

I think no one can accuse me of being partial to either of the classes reviewed. If the materialist says, "You have nothing tangible or palpable to offer us," I answer, neither is gravity nor evolution tangible, yet you believe both. To the religionist I would say, if apparitions and spiritual manifestations were good to found a religion on eighteen hundred years ago, why are they not good to confirm it in these latter days? To the spiritualist I would say, you can afford to be patient of skepticism and tolerant of criticism; for if your claims are true, your triumph is only a matter of time.

—*1880.*

IN MEMORIAM.

Brother W. A. Haskin has passed to the higher life. It seems proper that one who loved him well and appreciated his character should write a few words to his memory.

From the early part of his sickness he was conscious that the end of his earth life was approaching.

During my acquintance, extending back fifteen years, he has been a firm spiritualist. The faculties of his mind were so mixed and blended that he was not troubled with those doubts which intrude, unbidden, on others.

During the only brief conversation I had with him during his sickness he said: "I have done the best I knew how; I have not intentionally injured any one; I am not afraid to die, and I do not believe in a blood atonement."

He was singularly free from the greed of gain, and loved peace and righteousness, as was manifest in his official services. He loved music, and was always ready to give his services to aid that branch of religious exercises. And now, as his end approaches, methinks I could hear him say:

> "I have been almost home; I may not tell,
> For language cannot paint what I have seen.
> The vail was very thin, and I so near,
> I caught the sheen of multitudes and heard
> Voices that called and answered from afar
> Through spaces inconceivable, and songs
> Whose harmonies responsive surged and sank
> On the attenuate air till all my soul
> Was thrilled and filled with music, and I prayed
> To be let loose that I might cast myself
> Upon the mighty tides and give my life
> To the supernal raptures; ay, I prayed
> That death might come and give me my release
> From this poor clay, and that I might be born
> By its last travail into LIFE."

And then comes the separation of the spirit body from the physical body—for there is a spiritual body. Commencing at the feet, the spirit gradually withdrew from the nerves of organic life, and at length the attenuated particles escaped from the useless body through the upper portion of the skull, which in infants is unclosed. When the spirit is separated and has gathered the needed electric, magnetic, and other life elements, it may be seen by the clairvoyant eye reclining on the ambient air, palpitating with perennial life and glowing with more than youthful vigor, grace, and beauty. He is now prepared to walk the shining shore with the host of happy ones already there, and grapple with the problem of spirit life.

To his life-long companion I would say, Mourn not, he is not dead, but gone before; in a few short days you and I will pass the dark river and meet him there. The darkness will be but momentary, and on that shining shore your mother and husband will meet you with outstretched arms and greet you with kisses more rapturous than those that thrilled you at your betrothal fifty-three years ago.

> And as you join the angel throng,
> And countless ages march along,
> Your love shall glow still unabated
> As when your youthful hearts were mated.

—1881.

NAPA VALLEY.

BY J. ALLYN.

Of all the lands in east or west,
I count the Napa vale the best.
With Nature's gifts 'tis ever teeming;
The genial sun is ever beaming;
The best of Nature's gifts abound,
And healthful breezes fan the ground;
No wild tornadoes devastate,
Nor parching droughts to desolate;
Grapes abound in generous measure,
And Ceres strews her gifts at leisure.

There is a legend of an Italian nobleman who had his beautiful villa profusely adorned with fountains, statues, cypresses, flowers, and rare shrubbery, but, as happens to all in due course of nature, he was laid upon his death-bed. The padre came to console him and fit him for the great change. He pictured to him the beauties of Paradise, the ravishing music of the angels with their golden harps. Uneasily he turned his face to the wall and said, "I do not want to exchange; this is good enough for me," and closed his eyes for the last time.

—*April 1, 1881.*

GOD.

NUMBER FOUR.

I am a Pantheist; I know no God but Pan—the entirety of the universe—the All.

I shall express my views on this theme as fully and explicitly as I may, without the least hesitation or trepidation, though realizing that some of our sharpest critics have been eagerly nibbing their pens to review what may be offered. Although these views have served as a comfortable cushion on which to rest my soul, wearied with other ologies and isms; still I am wedded to no theory, anchored to no conception. If a horticulturist can show me a cherished error in regard to the growth of plants and trees in my garden, or impart a new truth, I regard him as a benefactor. Why should one who removes an error or imparts a truth on the greatest of themes be regarded in any other light? Neither am I so silly as to suppose that God will, of positive volition and purpose, punish me here or hereafter, for entertaining an error on a subject wherein the best minds ever matured on this planet could have conceived but a mere fragment of the whole truth, and probably cherished many errors. God favors those most who know and harmonize themselves with most of His laws, expressed in that part of the universe we inhabit; and, having used due diligence, our comprehension is limited by our capacities, which were given by powers wholly above and beyond ourselves.

I make no claim to originality; these views have been substantially entertained by philosophers more than a thousand years ago; and, two hundred years ago, a physically diminutive Englishman, of poetic and mediumistic mind, expressed the gist of the matter in beautiful language:

"All are but parts of one stupendous whole,
Whose body Nature is, and God the soul;
That, changed through all, and yet in all the same;
Great in the earth, as in th' ethereal frame;
Warms in the sun, refreshes in the breeze,
Glows in the stars, and blossoms in the trees;
Lives through all life, extends through all extent;
Spreads undivided, operates unspent;
Breathes in our soul, informs our mortal part,
As full, as perfect in a hair as heart;
As full, as perfect, in vile man that mourns,
As the rapt seraph that adores and burns;
To Him, no high, no low, no great, no small;
He fills, He bounds, connects, and equals all."

It is assumed that man occupies, comprehends, and sees, even with the most powerful instruments, but a mere fragment of the universe, relatively a mere point in space; and that, by the utmost stretch of the imagination, he comprehends an equally small relative point in time. The more wide his observations, the more fully is it shown that the same or similar elements abound, and that the same laws, or orderly sequence of effects after causes, obtain; indicating that the WHOLE is a UNITY. The substance, entities, elements both palpable and impalpable must be of the substance and laws of that vast Unity which I term God. If God does not comprehend the whole, there must be a portion outside of Himself without any God; or there must be a plurality of Gods; either of which suppositions derogates from the most approved characteristics of such a Being.

I sometimes say in public speaking, "God loves His creatures, especially man in rudimental and spirit life—the highest creature evolved on this planet." This is simply popular language; when translated into philosophical terms, it might read: "The elements, laws, and life-giving forces of this earth converged and wrought together for countless ages to produce the crowning fruit of the tree of life—the human spirit; and they will still work together for ages to complete what is begun in man; plainly indicating that 'the perfection of the human spirit is the secret intention of nature.'" Incompleteness of expression, adapted to popular assemblies of children and adults, is admissible, if not inevitable. Thus we say, "The sun rises in the east and sets in the west, traversing the visible heavens in about twelve hours;" speaking more philosophically, we should say, "The sun is the center of the solar system, and is relatively a fixed point; the earth turns round on its axis once in twenty-four hours, causing the phenomena of day and night."

Then the laws, or method of orderly sequence, of that fragment of the universe within the pale of human observation—elementary substance, gravitation, mathematical principles, chemical laws, vital forces, electrical laws, spiritual laws, and all other laws and principles, occult or palpable, known or unknown, knowable or unknowable—are the laws of God. Such of these laws as are definitely formulated and recognized by cultivated men, may be said to be known; beyond these, in the vast sea of the unknown portion of Deity, whoever presumes or guesses should not dogmatize, or ask others to believe, as there are a thousand chances of error to one of truth.

I am inclined to think that, as all matter constitutes the visible body of Deity, a small fragment of which assumes the globular form in our earth, and a still smaller part is articulated to form the human body, for the use and development of the indwelling spirit during its rudimental existence; so there is a vast, boundless sea of mind constituting the soul or spirit side of Deity; and but a minute fragment is localized, finitized, and adapted to use, in the human spirit. Between God and man there is no standard of comparison, no parallel, no principle by which one can be judged by the other; the absurd maxim, that man was created in the image of God, only leads to a wilderness of errors

As I am unwilling to trespass on your columns, other articles will be required to illustrate and prove this postulate, and more to follow.

Eight articles were published, but are lost.—J. A.

SPIRITUALISM THE RELIGION OF NATURE.

NUMBER ONE.

Old theologians, bigoted sectarians, and even those who are in a slight degree dependent on the popular churches for spiritual development, salvation, or religious culture, are requested not to read this article. It is written expressly for the benefit of spiritualists, progressionists, and liberal thinkers. And let me bespeak the patience and toleration of such, while I address you a few plain words upon the gist of the matter which we are holding out to the world as of paramount importance. Twenty years ago the writer left the church, because she would not tolerate the utterance of what to him appeared as vital truth. I trust he will not be forced to come out from spiritualists for the same reason.

Probably the majority of spiritualists regard this whole movement as simply a disintegrating power, whose end and object is to level to the ground the churches, show the absurdity of an authority in Scripture given by supernatural inspiration, and the utter unsoundness of the theology of Christianity. Having satisfied themselves by a careful study of the phenomena, that, after the change called death, our existence is continuous under the laws of our being and surroundings; they conclude there is no eternal hell, heaven is sure, and they prefer to take their own time and way of reaching that delectable place, without being at too much trouble and expense to facilitate the journey, or assist others in reaching their inevitable destiny. If it were an isolated case, it might not be significant that friends vociferously insist, in the " Fraternity Conference," that spiritualism is nothing but a disintegrating power, while many firm spiritualists, with their families, resort to a free Unitarian church for spiritual pabulum.

A clear-headed writer on the Religion of Nature says: "'Do not destroy or tear down religion, if you cannot substitute a better in its place' is the cry which meets the religious iconoclast continually; as if it were his or any one's duty to manufacture a religion for the people; as if nature, which gave us birth and sustains us, and is a sufficient guide in scientific pursuits, in our every-day labors, in health and disease, and in our political organizations, should fail us in our social, moral, and spiritual relations!"

A thorough and intelligent spiritualist, who has given liberally of his time, his influence, and his money to the good work, put the question, as near as memory serves me, in this manner: "Do you consider the religions of mankind, as developed in history, to be an excrescence, an intrusion, foisted on the ignorant many by the designing few for their own selfish aggrandizement, or a natural, normal growth, like governments, which, though imperfect, have supplied an imperious need of humanity, and which were as perfect in every age and country as the development of the people would permit?"

It must be plain to every reflecting mind, that, if the former is true, all that is requisite for the highest interest of humanity is to utterly demolish all religions from the face of the earth; if the latter, then the more difficult problem is presented to the reformer, of showing the errors of the old and substituting a better in its place.

"The master must become the builder too."

That man is a part of nature—if we use the term to include the spiritual, the imponderable, as well as the palpable—and that his physical, intellectual, and spiritual powers are developed, and ever must exist, under her beneficent laws and forces, is a proposition so self-evident to an instructed mind, as scarcely to need discussion. But this seems as far as most spiritualistic writers go, ignoring the great fact that the real problem pressing upon this age, and indeed, upon every age, for solution, lies beyond this. Your correspondent, after beautifully elucidating the subject up to this point, complacently stops, as if the subject were exhausted and nothing more need be said or done.

To me, it appears that they have just passed the vestibule, and scarcely entered the temple of religious truth and culture. None but the exceedingly ignorant at this day doubt that agriculture, horticulture, mechanics, and other fields of human effort and achievement, are developed under nature's laws; but so long as but a part of these laws are known, and a still smaller part controlled to man's purposes, there must be a continued progress as human intellect and will are brought to bear upon them. For a religious iconoclast, while with herculean blows demolishing the prevalent religions, to complacently ignore any obligation upon him, or any one else, to substitute a better in its place, is much as if a writer on civil government should say to his fellow-citizens, "There is no obligation resting upon you to manufacture a government for the public, or to substitute better laws for the bad ones you are exerting yourselves to get repealed. Supernatural powers, either malevolent or benevolent, have nothing to do with governments; laws are made by men; men are a part of nature, and nature will take care of herself." But the question still recurs; and for ages will recur, What is nature? What are her laws, teachings, and requirements? An ancient mythology represents a sphinx as propounding riddles to those who approach her. If they are able to solve them it is well; if not: she devours them. Nature is continually presenting this sphinx-riddle to individuals, to nations, to religions; if they solve it correctly, it is well; if not she devours or at least mangles them. Admitting that man's intellectual, spiritual, and executive powers are parts of nature, it remains to ascertain what are the functions and uses of these powers in promoting the moral and spiritual development of the race and of individuals. It is a favorite theory with many, that when humanity attains the maturity of its development on this planet, there will be such a growth of the intellectual and moral faculties as to preclude the use of the learned professions; every man will be a law unto himself, his own priest, king, and physician. Some writers seem to leap over the immense chasm of time separating this condition from the present, especially when treating of the subject of religion, which may be defined as the best method and means the human intellect has been able to devise and put in practical operation for the moral and spiritual culture of the race.

Spiritualists hold that civilized nations are sadly in need of a new religion. It is true that the practical workings of the churches (thanks to native common sense) are better than their creeds and their theology; but the striking discrepancies can but have a damaging effect.

—1867.

THE NEED OF A NEW RELIGION.

NUMBER TWO.

It is well understood by those who look beneath the surface, and scan the undercurrents of religious and intellectual life, that in religious development, we are now in a *transition period*. These transition periods occur alike in the physical, intellectual, political, and religious unfoldments. In the physical world, they mark the separation of the several planets from their parent suns, the satellites from their planets, and the point separating the close of one geological formation, or epoch, and the beginning of another. In politics, they mark the beginning and end of parties, nations, and particular systems of governments. Sir Charles Lyell has labored to show that these changes from one geological epoch to another were not produced by any extraordinary causes or great convulsions, but by the gradual operation of such causes as are in constant operation. However this may be, the separating lines are strongly marked,

There is a striking analogy between the physical progressions and formations, and those of the religious or spiritual. The mosaic period may be defined as commencing with the escape of the Hebrews from Egyptian bondage; and, as applied to a people and a country, to have ended with the advent of the Christian era, and the destruction of Jerusalem by the Romans; though it remains to this day the religious system of a scattered people. The advent of Christ was the beginning of the Christian era; and the transition period may fairly be considered to extend over the first three centuries thereof.

Some six centuries after Christ, Mahomet made his appearance, marking the beginning of a religious era of no mean importance. Mahometanism spread with great rapidity, and at length threatened to overrun western Europe, until Charles Martel met their war-like hosts on the bloody plains of Poictiers and drove them back; and, after long and cruel wars, the Mahometan Moriscos were driven from Spain. A celebrated historian sagely remarks, had the result of this battle been the reverse, perhaps the Mohametan mosque would now be glittering in the place of Christian cathedrals in western Europe.

I now write under the settled conviction that a new religious epoch is initiated, based on reason, science, and the positive facts of man's existence, relations, and needs; and that, as this epoch shall be unfolded, enough of the spirit's future life, and of its happiness as the sequence of religious culture, will be exhibited, to indicate, perhaps demonstrate, the importance of a system of religious training and culture, which shall become as substantially and truly national as was ever any religion in any age or country. Many, who have been accustomed to external vision, will not perceive that we are in such a transition period. These changes are slow, compared with the life of man, and not coming at first with outward signs of observation, are not readily perceived by external vision. Probably as great a proportion of the people now read correctly the signs of the times, as perceived the transitional character of the period during the initiation of Christianity. For three centuries, the fathers of the Church maintained an unequal struggle with polytheism. During this time, the Christians were a hated, despised, persecuted sect. The Proconsul Pliny had the candor to acknowledge the industry, honesty, and law-abiding character of the Christians; but this is more than many others were willing to allow. "For the most part," says the historian Tacitus, "this pernicious superstition (Christianity) was suppressed, but it broke out again; not only over Judea, whence it sprang, but in the city of Rome also, whither do run all the shameful and flagrant enormities." At length the Roman Emperor Constantine was converted to Christianity in the fourth century, when the Christians, being triumphant, turned and persecuted the polytheists and demolished their temples. If the transition from Judaism and polytheism to Christianity occupied over three centuries, it is scarcely reasonable to expect that the transition from Church Theology to Progressive Harmonialism will occupy less than one century, notwithstanding the more general diffusion of education, the great facilities of travel, the general advancement of science, and the power of the printing press.

All who study transition periods, in religious or intellectual development, will find unequivocal characteristics strongly marked. In such times it will be seen that the best minds, the deepest thinkers, have lost confidence in the basic philosophy of the departing epoch. There is a general quickening of intellect, and positions, long considered settled, are boldly questioned. Some frankly avow their sentiments, and even their thoughts; but many, trammeled by their professions or social relations, studiously conceal both. When Paul visited Athens he found an audience who did nothing else but hear or propound some new thing. The decaying systems of polytheism and Grecian philosophy proved a fertile soil for Christianity, when zealously uttered with undoubting confidence.

The world is still young and man in his early youth, as is indicated by the rapid progress of humanity in scientific knowledge and general intellectual development. The system of religion heretofore in vogue, like the temporary teeth of childhood, incapable of that expansion requisite to adapt it to the uses of maturity, must, from its roots upwards, like the temporary teeth, be absorbed away, and simultaneously substituted by a permanent growth, adapted to the uses of mature manhood. There is a beautiful analogy throughout nature's processes, great and small, palpable and impalpable, physical and spiritual.

The original and inquisitive character of the American people will not permanently abide religion received at second-hand. Our religion, like our government, must be indigenous to the soil; adapted to the peculiar character of our people, the genius of our institutions, and capable of future growth and expansion, like other sciences. It must aim to develop, individualize, and render self-poised and independent each individual soul. In doing this without trenching on the inalienable right of free thought, investigation, and belief, it must put in play a vigorous system for the moral and religious culture of children, and the rest of mankind, who are children of a larger growth. It must be the peculiar duty and pleasure of the ministers of religion, to enlarge the boundaries of religious science. The

Church, instead of frowning at all inquiries concerning our spiritual nature and future life, should approve of such interrogatories, made in a proper spirit, though the result should vary from the dictum of an antique book. Here lies the weakness of old theology; it assumes an infallible standard not based on science; the continued progress of which is continually undermining its foundation, putting the clergy to disingenuous shifts to prevent the superstructure from tumbling about their ears.

DASHAWAY HALL.

INTERESTING LECTURE ON ASTRONOMY — THE LATEST THEORY OF ASTRONOMERS ON THE LIGHT AND HEAT OF THE SUN.

At the regular weekly meeting of the Dashaways, held Sunday evening at their hall, there was a large attendance. The chief attraction of the evening was a lecture by John Allyn of Oakland on "The Modern Achievements of Astronomy."

The lecturer briefly traced the progress of astronomical science from the time of the shepherds of Chaldea through the clumsy theories of the Egyptians and the philosophers of Greece to the demonstration of the Copernican theory by Newton. He then gave an account of later speculations concerning interesting astronomical phenomena.

He said once every thirty-three years there occurs a meteoric shower of great extent and brilliancy. The latest theory of astronomers concerning these showers may be stated thus: There is a belt, composed of small masses of matter weighing for the most part but a few ounces each, which revolves around the sun in a form similar to the orbits of the planets, and is in composition similar to those larger meteors which penetrate our atmosphere and reach the surface of the earth. This belt revolves at the rate of eighteen hundred miles a minute. The earth moves with an equal velocity, and when one of these masses of matter encounters our atmosphere, the great velocity causes it to ignite, and we call it a meteor.

The earth in its revolutions each year passes through this belt, and the masses of matter meeting the atmosphere in greater or less number, a meteoric shower of greater or less brilliancy is formed. The meteoric matter is not distributed equally throughout the belt, but is concentrated very much at one point, which is called the node. In the revolutions of the belt this node is brought into the pathway of the earth once in thirty-three years, and the great number of meteors then formed constitute a shower of much greater brilliancy than at other times. The superior mass of the earth attracts many of the small masses of matter out of their regular courses, and a greater number than lie in the immediate course of the earth are made to fall into its atmosphere; thus the extent and brilliancy of the shower is increased. These meteoric masses rarely reach the surface of the earth, being generally consumed before penetrating the atmosphere to within fifty miles of the earth's surface.

Taking the hint from this phenomenon, Mayer, a profound German philosopher, boldly propagates a theory, which has been received with favor by astronomers, that the light and heat of the sun are caused by meteors falling upon the sun's atmosphere. The mass of the sun being so immense, it attracts to itself the small meteoric masses which exist not only in the belt before spoken of, but also throughout the solar system, and perhaps interstellar spaces. The sun being so much more ponderous than the earth, attracts so many more of the meteoric bodies that, while the earth has an occasional "falling star," a shower of meteors is constantly maintained upon every portion of the sun's atmosphere, giving light and heat to all the planets.

The atmosphere of the sun extends several thousand miles from the sun's surface. It may be, therefore, that while this process of the combustion of meteoric matter is taking place in the upper portions of the atmosphere, only so much light and heat may reach the sun's surface, through clouds and haze, as serve to produce and support vegetable and animal life in great perfection.

The invention of the spectroscope opened a new field of investigation for the astronomer. By its aid it has been ascertained that not all of the nebulæ are resolvable, some of them being of gaseous composition. It is also demonstrated by means of this instrument that the sun and stars contain many of the material elements in common with the earth. By means of the spectroscope, new proof is brought to the demonstration of the nebular theory, that the planets were formed from matter originally in a gaseous state.

The lecturer explained the latest theories regarding the formation of the solar system and the production of organized life, quoting from professors Mitchell, Huxley, and others. He was listened to with much interest and received appreciative applause.

At the close of the lecture Mrs. Phelps read Whittier's "Pipes at Lucknow," and several ladies and gentlemen voluntered songs.

The meeting was closed by an address by the president upon the objects of the Dashaway Association.—*Bulletin.*

SCIENTIFIC ASSOCIATION.

EDITOR TRANSCRIPT:—Please insert the following plea for a scientific association in Oakland, whose object shall be to assist the members to acquire a knowledge of such natural science as is already achieved, as well as to add to the common stock. It seems as if the times were ripe for the initiating of such an association in this Athens of the Pacific. It is not enough that there is an Academy of Science in San Francisco, or that this is the seat of the State University. The contemplated association would in no way conflict with the aims or uses of either of these institutions, but would be auxiliary to both; and would no doubt, be so regarded by parties in interest.

A little over two hundred years ago, some half dozen calm and thoughtful men in London, banded together and formed the " Royal Society for the Improvement of Natural Knowledge." The ends they proposed were stated by the founders thus: " Our business was (precluding matters of theology and State affairs) to discourse and consider of philosophical inquiries and such as related thereto, as physic, anatomy, geometry, navigation, natural experiments, with the cultivation of these studies at home and abroad." It was by this society that the method of Lord Bacon was applied to scientific pursuits, and the principle of Newton published to the world.

Professor Huxley says, "that if all the books in the world, except the philosophical transactions of this society, were destroyed, it is safe to say that the foundation of physical science would remain unshaken, and that the vast intellectual progress of the last two centuries would be largely, though incompletely recorded." Without dwelling too long, he also thinks that England's sanitary improvements by which the visitations of the plague have been stayed for two centuries, and that her triumph over the resources of nature in commerce, arts, manufactures, and mechanics, are largely due to the labors of the Royal Society.

I know that the difficulties in the cultivation of the physical sciences appear formidable now as they always have done. No small amount of application is requisite to read up the vast accumulations of modern science, and keep pace with the achievements of scientists. So much is being done in older and more favored localities, that it seems hopeless to achieve distinction, and mediocrity seems humiliating, however much it may benefit the individual, or pave the way for some future Newton, Davy, or Faraday.

But in California, where there are so many, who, in their several pursuits, have refused to recognize difficulties, it is presumed that there are those who will not be kept back by obstructions in their pathway. It is true that achievements made in Europe or the East will be rendered available to develop our material resources, but this will not develop local talent, or promote other interests to which wealth should be a means. The condition of our natural resources tends to develop monopolies. Our irrigating canals, mineral veins, railroads, and tule lands, all tend to build up gigantic fortunes on the one hand, and debasing poverty on the other. This wealth promotes an ambition for vain display and extravagant expenditure, damaging alike to morals and the general prosperity. Art and science are the natural and much needed counterpoises to this tendency, and in no place on this coast can they be fostered with greater facility than here. It is presumed that there is sufficient leisure, taste, wealth, and quenchless craving for knowledge to render such a movement a grand success. Many persons of scientific tastes would be attracted here by our mild and genial climate, were facilities afforded to indulge in this favorite pursuit, while not a few residents will leave our shores for places where greater opportunities are afforded. Some years ago it was argued that a good public library would, by its attraction of residents, increase the value of real estate many fold its cost; will not a scientific association do the same?

A SMART TRICK.

HOW A CAT INVEIGLES THE WARY RAT TO HIS DESTRUCTION.

A lady subscriber who noticed the item in the *Post* about the smart cat in Castle Bros.' store, asked a *Post* representative to come to her house and observe the cunning device of her cat in its war against the rats. The reporter went up to the house, and saw in the back yard a big Tom sunning himself near a tree. The boards around this tree had been cut, so as to give the tree a chance to grow. Through this aperture the rats were in the habit of emerging for the purpose of raiding the premises when the absence of a smell of cat assured them of impunity.

The lady took a bacon bone and threw it out in the yard. Immediately Tom got up, and taking the bone, carried it near the hole and began rolling on it and rubbing himself with it very industriously. After he had greased himself well, he left the bone near the hole, lay down in front of it and appeared to go to sleep.

"Now," said the lady, "he will stay there until dark and all through the night, and in the morning there will be half a dozen rats laid out behind him."

The reporter asked what he greased himself for, and the lady said: "You see, the rats smell him if he remains there in his normal condition, and won't come out; but the grease of the bacon bone kills the cat smell on him and the rats are deceived, and when they come out, attracted by the smell of bacon, he catches them. When he can get a venison bone his catch is enormous, sometimes as many as twelve rats being found dead in the morning. As soon as any of us get up in the morning, he will scratch at the door to be let in, and will, by his mewing, induce us to go out and see his handiwork. Come round and look over the fence as you go down to your office in the morning, and see how many prizes he has drawn in the rodent lottery."

The reporter passed by the back yard the next day, and sure enough, there lay seven dead rats, side by side, ready for inspection. And they say cats and the other lower animals have only instinct, and don't think.

CURIOUS PHENOMENA.

On Sunday, July 1st, a large audience in San Francisco witnessed phenomena which are worthy of record in the transactions of every scientific society in the civilized world; and lest this statement may seem exaggerated, the following statement of facts is penned: These phenomena occurred in the presence of Mrs. Reid of San Jose. The lady had two slates mounted with wooden frames, each about four and a half by seven inches. The lady would rub the slates clean, put a bit of pencil as large as a grain of wheat on one, place the other on top, and invite any one in the audience to take hold of one end of these slates with both hands, and she would hold the other end in the same manner. This would continue from one to five minutes, when the slates were opened and found to be partly covered with writing, intelligible, and pertinent to some one present, generally the party holding the slates. One message was as near like this as memory serves: "I am getting along well. I have outgrown the conditions surrounding me previous to the great change. Signed, 'Your Grandson.'" A man stepped forward who appeared like a business man of the world. He held the slates, which on opening contained this writing in a bold hand, quite different from that of other writing: "I am happy to meet you. Your old-time friend, Wm. C. Ralston." The man appeared to be confounded, but collecting his thoughts, he turned to the audience and said: "I am a skeptic as to everything I do not see demonstrated, but I have no longer doubts of that," pointing to the slates. It is not necessary to detail other examples. The writer was sitting close by and watched things closely, and is satisfied that trickery or fraud is out of the question as an explanation. It must therefore be done, as it purports to be, by the spirit of some deceased persons or by some law of mind wholly unknown to science, and even in direct conflict with the recognized laws of matter and mind. These phenomena can be repeated easily, as the writer has demonstrated through mediumship of three other parties, extending back eight years.

As a stimulus to ferret out the fact, law, and significance of these phenomena, I will give a hundred dollars in gold coin to any member of the Academy of Sciences, or any professor of the University of California, who will prove these phenomena to be done by trickery or fraud, or any law of mind or matter other than the spiritual hypothesis includes. A friend at my elbow, who is able to fill his engagements, says he will give a thousand dollars on the same terms.

ADDRESS TO SOUTHERN SPIRITUALISTS.

ATLANTA, GA., Aug. 1884.

DR. J. ALLYN—Dear Sir:

Your address to the Southern Association of Spiritualists was highly appreciated throughout the South.

G. W. KATES,
Editor *Light*.

The following letter from John Allyn, delegate from San Francisco, California, was read and ordered to be inserted in the records of the association:

Mr. President, Brothers and Sisters: Having been appointed by the Progressive Spiritualists Association of San Francisco a delegate to your meeting, I indulged in anticipations of a season of spiritual refreshment in the pure air and amid the magnificent scenery of your well-chosen location. In May I was at Knoxville and Chattanooga, but, like Moses on Pisgah, I viewed the promised land, but was not permitted to enter it. Without knowing the measure of your success, I shall congratulate you that you have secured so central and salubrious a location, which, I trust, will be held sacred to spiritual intercourse and culture long after its struggling founders have passed to the other side, still to work in this best of causes. In expressing my hearty wishes for your success and usefulness in promoting liberal and progressive thought, I feel that I am expressing the feeling of thousands scattered from the Atlantic ocean to

"Where the surging breakers roar
Along the grand Pacific shore."

Without pretending to the gift of prophecy, I feel impressed that an invincible host of spirits are now marshaling their forces to aid in a grand development of spiritualism in your section. To achieve the best results it is necessary that we who remain in the body should co-operate with them with wisdom, energy, and self-sacrificing devotion. Such is the condition of humanity, and particularly of religion and science, that we shall encounter determined opposition where we should receive kindly assistance; all things spiritual exist by virtue of immutable law, and the results of investigation promote all that is best and highest in religion. The scientist who denies spiritualism is confronted with facts which he cannot explain and which even go counter to his cherished philosophy. The religionist who denies it is ignoring the best evidences of his best doctrines, and surely playing into the hands of the bold materialist; therefore, the weakening and final capitulation of these two opposing forces is but a question of time.

Permit me to suggest that, to promote the best welfare of spiritualism, it is necessary to develop and encourage the best mediumship, and when found (a work in which the spirit world will co-operate) it is important that such mediums should be so sustained as to reduce to a minimum the temptation to mingle that which is genuine and useful with that which is otherwise—results which all intelligent spiritualists deplore—should be avoided by the kind and generous co-operation of all.

The social forces should be brought to our aid. We should encourage assemblies for spiritual culture with all the best means at our command. It is not enough that we get convincing evidence of a future life, but we should continue to grow spiritually until we pass out of the body with the full stature of men and women. Such an achievement is worthy of a life effort, and is the grandest fulfillment of earthly destiny.

We should do all in our power to promote personal liberty and freedom of thought. It is not possible that those who think at all should think alike or come to identical conclusions. The vain and hurtful creeds of the past should teach us to co-operate for the promotion of the good work, without trenching on the sacred right of individual liberty.

In conclusion, I would say that next to mediumship, the Children's Progressive Lyceum stands as a means of promoting true spiritualism and sound views upon religion. Let no effort be spared to maintain them whenever it is possible. Spiritualism is amenable to law as much as science, agriculture, or commerce. No seed falls upon good soil that will not germinate, and its fruitage will depend upon the culture it receives. Happy will be the soul which has been so interested in spiritual work, that on entering spirit life it will still be happy in working in the spiritual vineyard.

JOHN ALLYN.

St. Helena, Cal., July 8, 1884.

OUR PETRIFIED FOREST.

By DR. JOHN ALLYN.

Read at St. Helena Reading Club, August, 1883.

Within a few hours' ride of St. Helena are natural phenomena which, if they were in Europe, Egypt, or India, would be frequently visited by interested savants. I refer to silicified trees, known as the petrified forest. They differ materially from anything described by geologists. Professor Huxley visited a petrified forest in Egypt, which he thus describes:

"Every visitor to Cairo makes a pilgrimage to the petrified forest, which is to be seen in the desert a few miles to the north-east of that city; and indeed it is a spectacle worth seeing. Thousands of silicified trees, some of them thirty feet long and a foot or two in diameter, lie scattered about and partly imbedded in the sandy soil. Not a trunk has branches, or roots, or a trace of bark. None are upright. The structure of wood which had not time to decay before silification is usually preserved in its minutest details. The structure of these trees is often obscure, as if they had decayed before silification, and they are often penetrated, like other decayed wood, by fungi which, along with it, have been silicified.

"All these trunks have weathered out of miocene sandstone; and it has been suggested that when this sandstone was deposited, the Nile brought down great masses of timber from the upper country, just as the Mississippi sweeps down its rafts into the Gulf of Mexico at the present day, and that a portion of these, after long exposures and knocking about in the flood, became silted up in the sandy shore of the estuary. The greater part of the petrified forest is at present one thousand feet above the level of the sea, in the midst of the heights which form the eastern continuation of the Mokattam. It has therefore shared in the general elevation which took place after the beginning of the miocene epoch. That such elevation took place is proved by the marine beds of that epoch lying upon the upraised limestone plateau of upper Egypt."

In 1862 Professor Whitney passed up Napa valley, and made an extended geological survey at the expense of the State, but makes no mention of the petrified forest, although he passed within four miles of it. I can only account for this by supposing he did not know of its existence. It consists of a large number of trees, some of them five feet in diameter, completely petrified, even the roots and larger branches. Most of them lie prone upon the ground where they grew. They are quite unlike the petrifactions of Egypt, whose logs had been worn and battered in their passage from the upper waters of the Nile until the limbs, roots, and even the bark, were worn away. In one instance a trunk sixty feet long still stands in an upright position. Many of these trunks are broken square across in lengths of four to eight feet, showing the grain or rings and structure of the wood as plainly as if a tree had been cut in two with a saw, and then smoothed with a plane.

The soil is poor, of a cretaceous formation. It is supposed that petrifaction does not take place except where water can have free play to supply the mineral matter. The site of this forest is about one thousand feet above the level of the sea. The locality is hilly, indicating that great changes have taken place since these trees grew. They must have been in a basin which became filled with water until petrifaction took place, and the ground afterwards elevated to its present position. It is difficult to account for the trunks being broken across, except by their fall from an upright position after the trees were petrified. These petrifactions are semi-opal—by miners called wood-opal. Some of these are plainly of the redwood species. Professor Asa Gray says that the redwood forests of California are but the vanishing remnants that existed in earlier ages.

It is to be hoped that our legislators will make an appropriation so that we may have our geological survey completed, when we might expect a more complete account of this extraordinary phenomenon.

—*1880.*

MOUNT ST. HELENA.

In the museum of the geological survey is a copper plate, on which is engraved the name of Wasnessensky, a Russian naturalist, and the date, June 12, 1841. This indicates the date at which he ascended Mount St. Helena, and gave it this name in honor of the Empress of Russia. This is a volcanic mountain, from which volcanic material has spread east and southward. The height of this mountain, as measured by the coast survey, is 4,343 feet.

www.ingramcontent.com/pod-product-compliance
Lightning Source LLC
Chambersburg PA
CBHW020924230426
43666CB00008B/1558